Cane River Creole National Historical Park

Oakland Plantation

Gin Complex

Historic Structures Report

2004

Hartrampf, Inc.

and

Office of Jack Pyburn, Architect, Inc.

for

Historical Architecture, Cultural Resources Division

Southeast Regional Office

National Park Service

Cultural Resources
Southeast Region
National Park Service
100 Alabama St. SW
Atlanta, GA 30303
(404) 562-3117

The historic structure report presented here exists in two formats. A traditional, printed version is available for study at the park, the Southeastern Regional Office of the NPS (SERO), and at a variety of other repositories. For more widespread access, the historic structure report also exists in a web-based format through ParkNet, the website of the National Park Service. Please visit www.nps.gov for more information.

2004
Historic Structures Report
Gin Complex
OaklandPlantation
Cane River Creole National Historical Park
Natchitoches, LA
LCS#: 100635

Gin Complex, Oakland Plantation

Historic Structures Report

Approved by: _Laura Gates_ _4/16/04_

Superintendent   Date

Cane River Creole National Historical Park

Recommended by: _[signature]_ _5-20-04_

Chief, Cultural Resources   Date

Southeast Regional Office

Recommended by: _[signature]_ _5-20-04_

Associate Regional Director   Date

Cultural Resource Stewardship & Partnership

Southeast Regional Office

Concurred by: _[signature]_ _5-20-04_

Regional Director   Date

Southeast Regional Office

Table of Contents

Management Summary

Part I: Developmental History

Part II: Treatment and Use

Executive Summary

The Gin Complex at Oakland Plantation, Cane River Creole National Historical Park, Natchez, Louisiana is a part of one of the most complete collections of plantation structures in the possession of the National Park Service. The National Park Service acquired the property in 1998. Of the original Gin Complex structures, only the Seed House and the Cistern remain, though remnants of the engine mounts for the steam and diesel engines that powered the cotton processing machinery during the productive life of the Gin Complex can be seen at the site.

The Seed House was in an advanced state of decline at the time the National Park Service undertook stewardship of the site. The Park Service staff have since stabilized and rehabilitated the Seed House to facilitate converting it for use as a park maintenance facility. This report is intended to provide the historical background of the Gin Complex and the plantation that it served, to detail the existing condition of the remaining features and the probable configuration of those that are missing, and to provide recommendations for continued preservation and restoration of the Gin Complex features to enable the Park to make informed decisions regarding its use and maintenance.

Historical Summary

The major components of the Gin Complex at Oakland Plantation were first constructed between 1859 and 1861. They consisted of the Gin Barn, the Engine Building, the Seed House, and the Cistern. The Gin Barn contained a gin stand and an indoor, iron screw, box bale press. The Engine Building housed the boiler and the steam engine used to power the machinery in the Gin Barn. The Seed House, originally smaller than it currently is, was used to house the seed by-product of the cotton ginning process.

The Civil War brought few changes to the cotton processing procedure at the plantation. Shortly after the Civil War, a second gin stand was purchased, probably to augment the one already employed. The Gin Barn eventually contained two gin stands. By the 1890s, the Munger system of cotton processing had been invented and was employed by the Prud'hommes at Oakland Plantation. This required some changes to the structures of the Gin Complex. In addition to the new machinery in the Gin Barn, a seed-handling chute was installed from the Gin Barn to the Seed House. In the early 1920s, the steam

engine was replaced with a diesel engine. This involved the addition of a new Engine Room to the west of the Gin Barn. It may have been at this time that a new, up-packing hydraulic press was installed in the Gin Barn and the Seed House was expanded. The steam engine and the Cistern were abandoned.

In the early 1940s, the cotton crop was so poor that only seven bales of cotton were produced at Oakland Plantation. As a result, the ginning operations were closed. Thereafter, the Prudhommes took their cotton to the Starlight Plantation five miles away to have it ginned. The buildings fell into disrepair. At some point in the 1940s, the Gin Barn and Engine House were torn down, and the salvageable materials were reused to repair and rebuild other structures at Oakland Plantation. The equipment was either stored or sold.

The National Park Service purchased 44 acres of Oakland Plantation in 1998 for use as a National Park. After the General Management Plan for the proposed park was drafted and the Seed House, the only remaining structure of the Gin Complex, was designated a maintenance facility, the Park staff undertook extensive repairs to the building. These repairs are largely complete, with only the addition of restroom and storage facilities and the installation of permanent water, sewer, and electrical facilities remaining to be finished.

Architectural Summary

The Seed House at Oakland Plantation, with the Cistern and engine mounts, is the last vestige of a once bustling ginning operation. The Gin Barn was located just south of the Seed House, near the Cistern. The steam engine and boiler are located on the far side of the Cistern. The steam engine was the earliest power source for the gin. Later, a diesel engine replaced the steam engine and was positioned west of the Gin Barn. The Gin Barn housed two ginning stands and was fitted with Munger pneumatic cotton and seed handling equipment. The Munger system, in addition to extracting cotton from wagons for ginning, distributed cotton to the gin stands. After ginning the cotton, the system sent processed cotton to the press and the seed byproduct to the Seed House. Significant components of the Munger system remain in storage at Oakland.

The Cistern, located to the south of the Seed House, remains substantially intact. Its primary function was to provide water to the boiler. Its source of water, during the operation of the gin, was from the roof of the Gin Barn and Steam Engine House. Two sets of motor mounts remain on the site, the foundation for the steam engine to the south of the Cistern and the foundation for the diesel engine to the west of the Cistern. The mounts for the steam engine are masonry. The mounts for the diesel engine are concrete with brick chips as aggregate. This concrete dates to the dismantling of the boiler, which was located adjacent to the steam engine and covered in brick. The boiler was dismantled in the 1920s and the brick from the boiler shroud was reused in a variety of ways, including as aggregate for concrete used on the plantation.

Much change has taken place in the vicinity of the Seed House and the larger Gin Complex site since the National Park Service (NPS) acquired the property. Utilities have been brought in to the west of the Seed House. An above-ground gas tank and gravel parking have been installed to the southwest and north of the building, respectively. The area of the Gin Barn is presently being used for open storage. Currently, an outside contractor to the National Park Service is constructing a road leading from the Highway 494 to the Seed House.

The Seed House was in an advanced state of deterioration when the site was acquired by the National Park Service. In the General Management Plan, the proposed use of the structure was for "facility management". According to current park staff, this use includes maintenance staff operations and light woodworking activities.
The Seed House was constructed in two phases. The east and larger part of the existing structure was constructed first. This section of the building is a post-and-beam structure constructed from what appears to be recycled hewn timber material. Wire nails were the predominant method of attachment in the structure. However, larger, forged spikes were used at significant joints. No cut nails were observed. There are some interesting characteristics of the eastern section of the Seed House that deserve note. The floor of this section was originally designed to slope from the center to the outer walls on the long axis. It is thought by ginning experts and Prudhomme family members that this slope served to aid in distributing seed across the Seed House floor when blown in by the Munger system from the Gin House. The windows on the north and south sides of the Seed House were originally without frames or sashes but had bottom hinged shutters. The windows were used to control dust and, prior to the Munger system, to shovel seed into wagons from the north and south side of the Seed House.

The western portion of the structure was a later addition. It is all circular sawn wood and primarily accommodates a seed chute. Based on the configuration of the chute and a single wood Munger seed handling pipe hanging at the edge of the chute, it is clear the western segment of the structure was an expansion associated with the installation of the Munger system. The purpose of this modification was to more efficiently accommodate the ginning of cotton for both tenant farmers and community farmers living beyond the bounds of Oakland Plantation.

The Seed House has been altered considerably since its acquisition by the National Park Service. The building was stabilized by the reconstruction of all foundation piers. Where physically and structurally intact, existing beams and joists were retained, though supplemented in some areas to compensate for undersized historic members.

Most of the modification is related to adapting the Seed House for facility operations occupancy as prescribed in the General Management Plan. This involved:

- Removing the historic roofing, installing insulation and a waterproof membrane, and reinstalling the roofing in its historic location.
- Insulating the walls behind and, in some cases, in front of the historic siding. This treatment necessitated the installation of new finish material on much of the interior of the structure. Where appropriate, the National Park Service used material of the same species and dimension as the historic material lost to deterioration.
- Installing plywood flooring in lieu of the 4/4" floorboards that existed historically.
- Installing a unisex restroom in the northwest corner of the structure and a storage room to the east of the restroom. These spaces were not constructed to the full height of the building in order to retain a sense of the historic volume.
- Installing window frames, casement sashes and screens on the interior of the structure to provide light, as well as weather and insect protection.
- Installing plywood doors as a temporary treatment. The remaining plans call for the doors to be of board and batten construction typical of the plantation. Only the east horizontal sliding door existed when the property was acquired by the National Park Service.

In the long term, the General Management Plan designates the Seed House to be used for educational purposes. This use will support further interpretation of the seed handling operation of the Gin Complex as well as provide information about the Gin Barn and associated components of the complex. Every effort should be made to protect the remaining historic fabric and features of the Seed House. This will afford the maximum opportunity for accurate interpretation of the building, including the remaining components of the Munger system that are currently stored away from the Seed House.

Structural Summary: The restoration and rehabilitation of the Seed House is substantially complete. The General Management Plan defines the Phase I use of the Seed House as a Park maintenance facility. Discussions with Park personnel indicate that, although the building currently houses some carpentry equipment such as a table saw as well as some stored materials, the main use of the building will be as an office and assembly area for maintenance personnel. However, the reconstruction of the floor framing of the building, which was accomplished by replacing in kind the deteriorated portions of the floor framing and adding some supplemental strengthening, does not meet current building codes for loads in offices. In Phase II, the Park Service plans to convert the space for use as an educational facility when it becomes inadequate as a maintenance facility. What type of educational facility this would be is unclear. The floor framing as it currently exists does not meet current building code requirements for assembly areas, 100 psf, which it would be required to do if visitors were allowed to enter the building unrestricted. However, the load requirement for a classroom, which would include students, chairs, and desks, is 40 psf, the load the floor framing system can currently withstand based on the computer-modeled structural analysis of the system.

Two methods could be used to mitigate the problem of the floor framing not adhering to code with regard to the proposed uses of the Seed House as outlined in the General Management Plan. One is to strengthen the existing floor framing. This could be accomplished by strengthening it from below, or by adding an extra layer of plywood sheathing to strengthen it from above. It should be noted that much of the existing floor framing was installed between 1999 and 2002 by the National Park Service during rehabilitation efforts at the Seed House. Consequently, there is not a significant amount of remaining historic material in the floor framing system. Strengthening the floor framing from below would not result in any degradation of the existing visual presentation because all strengthening would be installed beneath the existing floor and would be, therefore, not visible to the casual observer. There

would be some expense associated with this approach. Strengthening it from above by adding additional plywood sheathing would impact the visual presentation somewhat, but would be much less expensive than strengthening it from below. According to Park personnel, the addition of an extra layer of plywood sheathin on the floor is planned for the Seed House. Because adding an extra layer of plywood sheathing to the existing flooring is the simplest to execute, less expensive than adding extra strengethening from below, and already part of the rehabilitation plans of the National Park Service for the Seed House, this is the preferred alternative. However, if the National Park Service decides not to add this additional layer of plywood, the floor must be strengthened from below to accommodate the proposed use.

The other method is to restrict the load on the floor framing. As it currently exists, the floor can withstand a load of 40 psf (pounds per square foot) based on the computer- modeled structural analysis of the framing. The code requirement for an office space is a load strength of 60 psf. To avoid strengthening the floor framing to meet current building codes, the Park must restrict the weight of stored materials and equipment to 40 psf. To do this, the Park will need to monitor the weight of items stored in the building as well as the weight and locations of office equipment such as desks, copiers, file cabinets, and lockers.

When the Park converts the Seed House to an educational facility, the building code requirements for public assembly space (100 psf) or for classroom space (40 psf) will apply. Which load applies depends on the configuration of the educational function of the building, whether as an assembly area with rows of chairs or as a classroom with desks. However, in both cases, restricting the number of people in the building can eliminate the need to strengthen the floor framing. To avoid additional strengthening of the floor framing, the number of people in the building should be limited to one hundred people, assuming maintenance equipment and storage has been removed.

This number would allow for the weight of folding chairs arranged for educational presentation purposes, or for desks and chairs arranged in rows, which, although weightier than simple rows of chairs, allows fewer people in the same area due to space restrictions. Park Service personnel would need to ensure that storage of educational equipment and supplies does not exceed 40 psf. If the floor framing is strengthened by the addition of another layer of plywood sheathing, the number of people that could be allowed in the building at one time could be raised to one hundred and fifty. It is unlikely that this building could physically accommodate one hundred and fifty people at one time, however.

A third means of reconciling the strength of the existing floor framing with the use of the building would be to change the proposed use to one that does not exceed the limits of the floor framing, such as a classroom, with students, desks, and chairs. However, this approach would require that the Park locate the current maintenance facility elsewhere, as the required load capacity for offices (60 psf) exceeds the existing load capacity of the floor framing system (40 psf).

Summary of Other Issues: It is not recommended that a permanent ramp be installed to facilitate handicapped access, as this will impact the historic presentation of the exterior of the Seed House and the Gin Complex as a whole. However, the Seed House could be made available for wheelchair access by the use of a portable access ramp. If a permanent ramp is desired, it should be located on the south side of the Seed House. Some historic components of the seed handling system still remain installed in the Seed House. It is recommended that these be retained and preserved and consideration be given to the reconstruction of as much of the seed-handling system as possible in the Seed House using existing stored materials supplemented by new construction. This would facilitate interpretation of the Seed House as it was originally used. Further archaeological investigation should be performed on the site. The foundations of the missing Gin Barn, Engine House, Boiler, Press, and Pit Scales could probably be discovered near the surface and should be excavated to further inform an understanding of the extent of these structures and their relationship to one another. The existing remnants, which include the Cistern, the engine mounts, and the various at-grade wall constructions and brick paving in the area of the Gin Barn should be preserved and maintained as part of the interpretive inventory of Oakland Plantation.

Recommendations for Treatment and Use:

- Preserve remaining historic features, including the east sliding door and hardware, the seed hopper and wood supply pipe, and the building's remaining historic wood components, including the heavy timber frame and remnants of wood sheathing.
- Relocate the facility maintenance operations to another locations better suited to its floor loading requirements.
- Consider reinstallation and reconstruction of the Munger seed handling system for interpretive purposes.
- Install an extra layer of ¾" plywood flooring on

top of the existing flooring, and restrict the number of people in the Seed House to one hundred and fifty people.
- If handicapped access is desired, install either a permanent ramp or a moveable ramp so that it accesses the south side of the building rather than the east side.
- Undertake further archaeological investigation at the site to attempt to uncover the foundations of the missing components of the Gin Complex, such as the Gin Barn, Engine Houses, Boiler, Press, and Pit Scales.

Administrative Data

Locational Data:

Building Name: Seed House and Gin Complex

Building Address 4386 Hwy. 494
Natchez, LA 71456
LCS #   91706

Related Studies:

Ford, Eric Z. *Design Analysis – Rehabilitation of the Seed House for Adaptive Reuse, Oakland Plantation.* National Park Service, U.S. Department of the Interior, 2001.

Jones, Tommy. *Gin Barn, The, Magnolia Plantation, Cane River Creole National Historical Park, Historic Structure Report.* National Park Service Southeast Region Support Office, Atlanta, 2002.

Keel, Bennie C., and Christina E. Miller, "Gabe Nargot's Cabin – Investigations at a Nineteenth Century Slave Domicile in Northwest Louisiana." Paper presented at 1999 Society for Historical Archaeology Conference, Salt Lake City. <http://www.cr.nps. gov/seac/gabes/ Dec. 15, 2000>.

Lawliss, L., C. Goetcheus, and D. Hasty, *"The Cultural Landscape Inventory and Assessment, Cane River Creole National Heritage Area Natchitoches, Louisiana."* National Park Service Southeast Region Support Office, Atlanta. 1997.

Miller, Christina E. and Susan E. Wood, *Oakland Plantation – A Comprehensive Subsurface Investigation.* Southeast Archaeological

Center, Tallahassee. 2000.
National Park Service. *Cane River Creole National Historical Park, Draft General Management Plan/Environmental Impact Statement.* 2000.

Cultural Resource Data:

National Register of Historic Places: The Jean Pierre Emmanuel Prud'homme Plantation (Oakland Plantation), historic structure, originally listed August 29, 1979 (upgraded from local to statewide significance August 2, 1989) under Criterion A for association with events that have made a significant contribution to the broad patterns of our history.

Period of Significance: The period of significance for Oakland Plantation begins with the founding of the plantation and concludes about 1960, around the time that the last of the sharecroppers and tenants were leaving the plantation.

Proposed Treatment and Use: According to the National Park Service General Management Plan for this park, the Seed house is to be used as a maintenance facility for the park. Discussions with park personnel indicate that this does not include moving heavy equipment such as backhoes and tractors into the building, but does include storage of the materials used to rehabilitate the building and the use of light equipment such as band saws and drill presses.

PART I: DEVELOPMENTAL HISTORY

Historical Timeline

1787 – Jean Pierre Emmanuel Prud'homme begins to farm lands along the Red (now Cane) River in Natchitoches Parish, Louisiana that would become Oakland Plantation.

1790 – Introduction of cotton as a cash crop in Louisiana.

1793 – Invention of the cotton gin by Eli Whitney.

1796 – Henry Ogden Holmes granted a patent for a "saw-toothed" gin, an improvement on the Whitney gin.

1799 – Whitney gins are first sold commercially.

1815 – End of the War of 1812; beginning of a cotton boom in the Lower South.

1836 – A contract is executed between William Miller and Lestan Prud'homme, Sr. to build "a gin house like Mr. Phanor Prud'homme's new gin house."

1838 – Daniel Pratt begins to manufacture gins at Prattville, Alabama.

1850 – Pierre Phanor Prud'homme purchases the Prud'homme plantation from his father's estate.

1850-1854 – Sometime during this period, Phanor Prud'homme installs a new, indoor, iron screw box press at one of the gin complexes at his plantation.

1854 – Raynond, a slave at Prud'hommes' Plantation, receives training from J.B. Clarkson at Union Plantation as a gin engineer (operator). Indicates either an existing or an impending steam-powered gin at Oakland Plantation.

1856 – Phanor Prud'homme arranges with P.B. Plauche and Co., his agent in New Orleans, to insure his two gins.
1857 – Phanor Prud'homme replaces a worn wooden screw of a screw press at one of his gins with a new one.

1857 – Phanor Prud'homme installs a Pratt gin at Prud'hommes' plantation.
1859 – For insurance purposes, Phanor Prud'homme values his two gins at $1500 for "mill on the side of the house," and $2000 for "mill on the side opposite the house," plus the value of cotton at both gins.

1859-1861 – Construction of New Gin, Engine Room, and Seed House on present site (only the Seed House survives).

1861 – Civil War begins at Ft. Sumter, Charleston, South Carolina.

1864 – Red River Campaign; destruction of gin.

1865 – End of the Civil War.

1867 – Gabe Nargot, gin engineer for Oakland Plantation born at Prud'hommes' plantation.

1873 – Formal division of the Prud'homme plantation results in Atahoe Plantation on the east side of Cane River and Oakland Plantation on the west side.

1885 – Invention of the "Munger system" of ginning by Robert S. Munger.

1885-1905 - Installation of this system at Oakland Plantation during this period probably prompted the expansion of the Seed House, which included the addition of a now-defunct seed pipe between the Gin Barn and the Seed House and the chute that still exists in the Seed House.

1920s – Gin steam engine replaced with diesel-powered engine.

1940/41 – "Bust" cotton crop.
1941/42 – New Gin closes, never to re-open.

1941-1957 – New Gin Barn torn down sometime during this period.

1950 – End of sharecropping arrangements on Oakland Plantation. Afterward, the Prud'hommes hired only day laborers.

1985 – Prud'hommes cease to farm and sell the majority of the farm equipment.
1998 – National Park Service acquires 44 acres of Oakland Plantation for a proposed National Park, the Cane River Creole National Historical Park.

1999 – National Park Service initiates stabilization and preservation measures for the Seed House. These measures included rebuilding the brick piers on concrete footings, replacing wooden grade-piers with new brick piers and footings, repairing or replacing some sill beams and floor joists, adding supplemental framing to level the floor, repairing the wall and roof framing systems, including some replacement of sheathing boards and rafters, reconstructing missing northwest and southwest lean-to roofs, and repairing the northeast lean-to roof.

2002 – National Park Service is currently undertaking modifications to the interior of the Seed House that include installation of restrooms and storage areas.

Historical Background and Context

No discussion of the dependent structures at what is now called Oakland Plantation can begin without first establishing, in brief, the background history of the plantation on which they stand and the people that erected them and put them to use. Much has been written regarding the Natchitoches Prud'homme family. They were among the first families of Louisiana when the territory belonged to the French. They continued to be one of the prominent families of the area through the subsequent occupation of the Spanish, the re-establishment of French control, and the acquisition of the territory by the United States government. The Prud'hommes established a successful agricultural enterprise and prospered despite the vicissitudes of economic forces and national politics. Two hundred years after the establishment of their plantation along the Cane River, they sold an important part of it to the National Park Service to establish a park that would serve to educate the public and preserve the remnants of a vanished way of life and a significant part of the nation's history.

The existing Seed House and the site of what was known to the Prud'hommes and their workers as the New Gin are an important part of that remnant. Farm records show the construction of a Gin Barn, Engine House, and Cistern on this site in 1859 through 1860. Work on a Seed House appears in records for 1861,[1] but it is not certain that this refers to the Seed House that currently exists at the site of the New Gin. This report explores the background history of the Prud'hommes' cotton plantation, the construction of the New Gin, and the modifications to both as times and technology changed.

By 1758, Jean-Baptist Prud'homme had acquired land along what was then called the Red River and begun to farm it. According to family tradition, his oldest son, Jean Pierre Emmanuel, was farming land that would become Oakland Plantation by 1787, though his residence in the early 1790s was still on a 51-acre tract opposite the post at Natchitoches. However, by the late 1790s, Emmanuel Prud'homme had purchased that property from Nicholas Rousseau, the original owner, and built a home on the banks of the river.[2] Here, Emmanuel Prud'homme and his workers raised first indigo and tobacco and, later, cotton.

There is a tradition among the Prud'hommes that Emmanuel was the first to bring cotton production to the area on a large scale. Though cotton was introduced into the region about 1790, the invention of the cotton gin by Eli Whitney in 1793 made the processing of large amounts of cotton feasible and promoted the adoption of cotton as the pre-eminent crop in Louisiana.[3] However, the invention was not initially available for the planter to purchase. Whitney's original plan was not to sell the machines themselves but to sell the services of the machines for a part of the ginned crop, about 40 percent. This plan did not succeed because planters objected to what they considered the exorbitant rate charged by the ginner and instigated attempts to steal the designs for the gins and build their own. It was not until 1799 that planters were able to buy Whitney gins for their own plantations.[4] During the 1790s, cotton was doubtless ginned by hand on the Prud'hommes' plantation, but Emmanuel Prud'homme probably purchased a mechanical gin as soon as possible. By 1803, cotton had largely replaced tobacco as the primary cash crop in the Natchitoches area.[5]

After the War of 1812 ended in 1815, the production of cotton became increasingly profitable, as the price per bale increased. The average price for cotton in 1815 was an almost unbelievably high 29.4 cents per pound. By 1817, it had peaked at 33.9 cents per pound.[6] The cotton boom in the area led to an increase in production by the large plantation owners, and the resulting affluence produced the legendary culture and society of the antebellum South. As historian Anne Malone points out, this increased prosperity resulted in the building of "bigger and more luxurious houses, barns, stables, and quarters…."[7]

The production of cotton on the Cane River plantations was greatly facilitated by the excellence and depth of the soil, the result of centuries of flooding cycles. However, the vicissitudes of weather tempered the output. In 1836, it appears that Prud'hommes' plantation produced more than 990 bales of cotton (based on the weight of picked cotton recorded by the overseer – prior to the Civil War, a

---

[1] Anne Patton Malone, "Oakland Plantation, Its People's Testimony," unpublished MS, National Park Service, 1998, p. 62.
[2] Ibid., pp 24-26.

[3] Ibid., pp. 31-32.
[4] Karen Gerheardt Britton. *Bale o'Cotton, The Mechanical Art of Cotton Ginning*, Texas A&M University Press, College Station, 1992. pp. 17-19.
[5] Caroline Breedlove. "Bermuda/Oakland Plantation, 1830-1880." Unpublished masters thesis. Northwestern State University of Louisiana, Natchitoches 1999. p. 54.
[6] Malone, pp. 36-41.
[7] Ibid., p. 48.

400-pound bale was standard). The drought of 1838 resulted in only 327 bales. In 1850, only 210 bales were produced, but the inventory of Lise Prud'homme's succession in 1853 showed 500 bales. In 1860, Prud'hommes' plantation produced 628 bales in spite of a severe drought that destroyed much of the cotton crop in north central Louisiana.[8]

Before the Civil War, cotton was hand-picked by slave laborers at the Prud'hommes' plantation. The workers hauled woven baskets or sacks of heavy cotton duck between the rows to hold the cotton they picked. Some of the stronger men used a sack twelve feet long. A sack of cotton could weigh up to 300 pounds, depending on the size of the sack, the length of the rows being picked, the quality of the cotton crop, and the distance to the weigh station located in the cotton field.[9] The plantation overseer recorded the amounts picked for each worker. For instance, in October of 1836, "the overseer Culbertson recorded women like Big Liza, 'Sucky,' Betsy, and 'Tonet' as having picked 200 pounds or more, keeping pace with Charles, Lewis, Phil, and Alexan.... Again in 1860, on August 22, when four men were able to pick

Figure 1. Model of Whitney gin, ca. 1800. (from *Bale o' Cotton* by Britton)

over 300 pounds, so too did two of the women, with another two picking 280 and 285."[10] This was not the norm, however. The general wisdom was that a man could pick between two hundred and four hundred pounds of cotton a day. A woman could pick one hundred to one hundred and twenty-five pounds, with one hundred and fifty pounds being the maximum one could expect of women workers.

Pregnant women or nursing mothers could not be expected to pick more than a child could normally pick. Children, who were sent to pick cotton as early as eight years of age, could be expected to pick thirty to forty pounds per day.[11] When the container was full, or the worker could no longer drag it along, the cotton was weighed on the field scales and emptied into a wagon. Workers driving wagons pulled by mules transported the cotton to the gin for processing.[12] One wagon-load generally equaled one bale of cotton.[13]

Picking, ginning, and pressing, or baling, of cotton were performed simultaneously. As enough picked cotton was accumulated, it was ginned and baled. The work started in late August and picking usually finished by the end of the year. Sometimes, however, depending on weather, workers were still picking cotton in February.[14] The fields were usually picked more than once because the bolls did not all ripen at the same time. Ginning often did not end until March, the start of the planting season for the next crop of cotton.[15]

The heart of the cotton plantation was the cotton gin. The term "cotton gin" had two meanings. Used generally, it meant the entire facility that processed cotton. This included the cotton ginning machine, the cotton press, the buildings that housed the machinery and stored the raw materials and finished product, and the supporting machinery and constructions, such as the devices, both manual and mechanical, that powered the machinery, the cistern, and the systems used to transport materials from place to place. Used specifically, it referred to the machine that separated the cotton fibers from the seeds by pulling the cotton fibers apart with combs mounted on revolving cylinders, also called a "gin stand." By 1836, "a belt-driven gin stand...must have stood upon the left bank"[16] (opposite the Main House side of the Cane River). In 1850, when Phanor Prud'homme purchased the plantation from his father's estate, there were two gins, one on each side of the river, to facilitate ginning on both portions of the plantation without having to haul cotton across the river.[17] At that time, there was no bridge, though there is evidence that they used or built "pontoon bridges" to cross from one side to the other. Before 1850, the gins were apparently powered manually, but, by 1854, at least one of the gins was converted to

---

[11] John Batten, to Ann Patton Malone in oral interview, 20 April 1997, transcript, p. 34.
[12] Prudhomme, Kenneth, 11 March 1997. pp. 13-15.
[13] Britton, p. 24.
[14] Prudhomme, Kenneth, 11 March 1997. p. 16.
[15] Britton, p. 27.
[16] Breedlove, p 76.
[17] Numerous references exist in the plantation records to "gin this side" and "gin other side," indicating a gin located on each side of the river.

steam.[18] From Phanor's correspondence, this appears to have been the gin on the side of the river opposite the Main House.[19]

In addition to the gin machinery, each plantation gin complex included a bale press. By the 1830s, wooden screw presses were widely used throughout the South, usually powered by draft animals. In the fall of 1838, Phanor Prud'homme made reference to the six mules and six horses then powering the Prud'hommes' press.[20] At that time, the cotton press was usually housed in a free-standing structure adjacent, but not attached, to the gin building. This arrangement was inherently inefficient, especially during inclement weather.

The steam-powered cotton gin, which included both the gin and pressing machinery as well as facilities for housing the machinery and for the storage of cotton, was an industrial enterprise. It was marked by a tall chimney of brick or sheet metal emitting steam or smoke, several buildings of brick or wood, the screeching sound of the cotton press, and the smells of lubricating grease and hot metal machinery parts.[21] This is a far cry from the bucolic landscape generally envisioned as the "southern plantation."

Operation of the gin required specialized knowledge. The Prud'hommes appear to have usually entrusted the operation of the gin to members of their work force. Between 1840 and 1860, a slave known as Arsen, or "Big Belly" was a gin operator.[22] He was probably operating the mule-driven gin. In 1854, one of the plantation workers, Raynond, was receiving training from John B. Clarkson of Union Plantation to run the new steam-powered gin.[23]

Cotton prices were high in the 1850s.[24] It was a time of optimism and expansion for the planters on Cane River. Phanor Prud'homme embarked on a number of construction projects intended to improve the plantation operations. Improvements to the ginning operations were among them. By the 1850s, presses that allowed for indoor operation were being patented. The advertisement of James L. McComb of Raymond, Mississippi for an indoor press that he had developed attracted the attention of Phanor Prud'homme, who wrote to him inquiring about it.[25]

By 1854, he had purchased and installed one of these presses, an iron screw box press, to replace one of the wooden presses.[26] This necessitated the construction of a new Gin Barn to house the indoor press operation in the same building as the gin operation. The combination of these operations in one building was a great step forward for the typical plantation because it allowed work to continue even in inclement weather. Farm journals record the installation of a Pratt's Gin in January of 1857. On the 26th of January, the plantation overseer, Seneca Pace, sent "5 men, 1 cart" to pick up the gin stand.[27] The following day, the gin stand was installed, and, on the 29th of the month, the gin was started at 10 in the morning. It may have been powered by the new

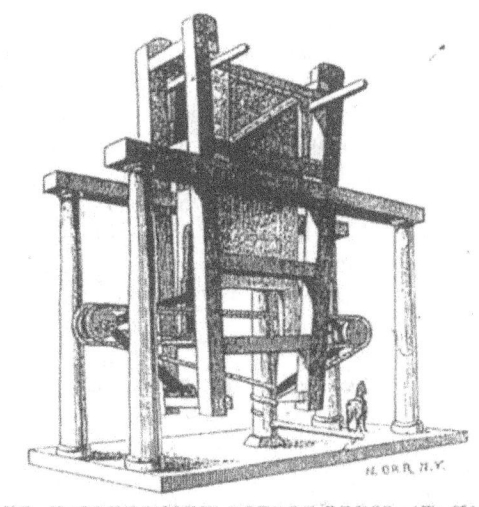

MR. McCOMBS' NEW COTTON PRESS.—(Fig. 39.)

Figure 2. Phanor Prud'homme apparently installed an indoor press such as this at Oakland in the 1850s. (from *The Southern Cultivator*, July 1850)

steam engine purchased by Phanor and run by the slave, Raynond, who had been trained in "gin engineering" in 1854. If so, the new Pratt's gin was installed in the gin on the other side of the river from the Main House.[28] Pace reported that the gin "performed well."[29] From April to July, timber was accumulated for the construction of gin buildings, and the buildings were begun at the end of July. Pace documented the progress and problems experienced in processing the cotton that year on both sides of the river. The problems were largely due to rainy weather, wet cotton, and a press in need of repair on

---

[18] Malone, p. 76.
[19] Ian Firth, "Cultural Landscape Report – Oakland Plantation," draft manuscript, n.d., n.p.
[20] *Ibid.*
[21] Breedlove, p. 77.
[22] Malone, pp. 74-75.
[23] *Ibid.*, p. 76.
[24] *Ibid.*, pp. 49-50.
[25] Phanor Prud'homme, letter to J. McComb, October 7, 1850, Series 3.1.1, folder 143, Prud'homme Collection #613, Southern Historical Collection, University of North Carolina at Chapel Hill, NC.

[26] Firth, n.p.
[27] Seneca Pace, 1857 Overseer's Farm Journal, Prud'homme Collection #613, Southern Historical Collection, University of North Carolina at Chapel Hill, NC, n.p.
[28] Firth, n.p.
[29] Pace, n.p.

Figure 3. Pratt's farm gin, ca. 1844. (from *Bale o' Cotton* by Britton)

the Main House side of the river.[30]

The plantation operated two gins throughout the 1850s. "In 1856, Phanor noted in his Journal that he had arranged for P. B. Plauche and Co., his agent in New Orleans, to insure his two gins. Two years later, when renewing his insurance, he valued the gins as follows. 'The mill on the side of the house for the sum of $1500 plus the value of 75 of picked and cleaned cotton. The mill on the side opposite the house is run by steam. You insured the steam engine for the sum of $2000. The cotton mill for the sum of $2000 and for the value of one hundred bales of picked and cleaned cotton…'"[31] However, by 1859, the construction of another gin and associated buildings was underway.

This new gin was located in a field south of the Overseer's House and west of the Quarters. By the end of 1860, Prud'hommes had three gins, one across the river, and two on the Main House side. The existence of several gins is documented in numerous references in the 1860 farm records. "For example, a January 14, 1860 reference by overseer Seneca Pace stated that cotton was hauled from the 'new gin' to the 'mule gin,'…. An entry for January 15, 1861 mentions moving cotton bales 'from gin to old gin.' And a February 16 [entry] mentions moving cotton from gin to old gin 'for shipping' (presumably because the old gin was close to the river). These are among many such references in the journals during the 1860s which indicate that the Old Gin and the New Gin existed at the same time."[32] However, not all of these gin buildings may have contained gin equipment. There is evidence in the farm records for the plantation that only two gins at a time contained gin equipment.[33]

The gin complex built in 1859 through 1861 consisted of a Gin Barn, a Seed House, and an Engine Building to house the boiler and steam engine used to run the gin. Between the Gin Barn and the Engine Building was a Cistern where water was accumulated to power the steam engine since the new gin was too far from the river to use the river water to supply water for the steam engine. The Gin Barn contained the gin stand and the indoor press equipment, both of which had been painstakingly hauled across the river from the gin on the other side.[34] On the eve of the Civil War, the Prud'hommes had two gins in operation on the plantation, at least one of them steam-powered, and both on the same side of the river as the Main House. If the Civil War had not intervened, they were poised to produce more cotton than ever before.

When the war broke out, the Prud'homme sons, Jacques Alphonse and Pierre Emmanuel II, enlisted in the Confederate Army.[35] In March of 1862, Alphonse was wounded. He was discharged from his unit and sent home to recuperate. He remained at the Prud'hommes' plantation until July of that year, when he and his brother-in-law, Winter Breazeale, recruited five companies of cavalry and set off in September to rejoin the war. However, in April of 1863, Alphonse was again wounded and obliged to return home to recuperate. By June of that year, he felt recovered enough to rejoin his unit. Still, he was mustered out of his unit in July of 1864 because of disability from the wounds that he had received and from which he had never properly recovered.[36]

Unable to continue as a soldier, Alphonse Prud'homme set about assisting his father, Phanor, with the management of the plantation. This was no small task, as the war had at last overrun "*la Cote Joyeuse.*"[37] The defeat of the Federal army at the battles of Mansfield and Pleasant Hill, north of Natchitoches, resulted in a retreat that led the Federal troops down the Cane (formerly, Red) River.

[30] *Ibid.*
[31] Firth, n.p.
[32] Malone, pp. 60-62.
[33] Ian Firth, Professor, School of Environmental Design, University of Georgia at Athens, Georgia, to Deborah Harvey, oral interview, 9 Sep 2002. This information is based on his research for the National Park Service in the Prud'homme papers held at the University of North Carolina at Chapel Hill, North Carolina.
[34] Firth, n.p.
[35] Breedlove, pp. 24-26.
[36] Alcee Fortier, ed., "Jacques Alphonse Prud'homme," *Louisiana, Comprising Sketches of Counties, Towns, Events, Institutions, and Persons Arranged in Cyclopedic Form,* Southern Historical Association, Atlanta, 1909, no page numbers.
[37] The name given to the Cane River Country by other Louisianans in the early 1800s. See DeBlieux, Robert B., *Cane River Country, "La Cote Joyeuse" and Kisatchie National Forest – An Auto Guide to the Historically and Architecturally Important Plantations of Creole Origins and a Guide to the Vistas, Hiking Trails and Flora of the Forest of Natchitoches Parish,* The Natchitoches Times, Natchitoches, 1993, p. 3.

Because the war made it impossible for Phanor Prud'homme to market his cotton, he was apparently storing it in an old gin near the river. Sometime during the Red River Campaign, the old gin was burned to the ground. Prud'homme family legend ascribes this event to the activities of the Federal troops.[38] Though they lost virtually all of their cotton to fire (only four bales escaped the blaze), and the old gin was destroyed,[39] the Prud'hommes were among the lucky. Unlike Magnolia Plantation, where the Main House was consumed by fire,[40] neither the Main House of the Prud'homme plantation nor most of the outbuildings were harmed during the retreat. Family tradition attributes this good fortune to the story that "faithful slaves begged the yankees [sic] not to burn the home."[41] Fortunately, the rest of the war was short. In May of 1865, the last of the Confederate Army surrendered.

Emmanuel Prud'homme II returned home to the plantation, and he and Alphonse undertook its management. Their father, Pierre Phanor, weakened by the demands of war, retired to the Lecomtes' townhouse in Natchitoches where he died on October 12, 1865.[42] His heirs, the Prud'homme brothers, and their families worked together to rebuild their lives.

Cotton continued to be the important cash crop for the plantation. In 1865, the price of cotton was posted at forty-one cents per pound, more than twice the price in 1863.[43] The Prud'hommes were fortunate in that, although their crop for 1864 had been destroyed, at least one gin with engine house and seed barn remained to them. Only the Old Gin near the river had burned, apparently leaving the New Gin largely intact. Still, in 1865, Phanor was able to plant only enough cotton to realize 21 bales at the end of the season.[44]

It appears that, though Prud'homme family legend states that the Federal troops burned only the old gin, they may have done some damage to another gin as well. Alphonse Prud'homme records in his journal that the steamer *Caddo* delivered a gin stand on the 11th of April of 1866. As there is no record of the construction of a gin after that of the New Gin, it may be inferred that this gin stand was intended to replace or augment one already in use. Prior to ginning season in 1866, it was apparently discovered that the press did not work and repairs were undertaken. In August, partially-ginned cotton had to be hauled to "town" (presumably, Natchitoches) to be pressed.[45] Farm records show that repairs were not begun until the middle of September of that year, when ginning season had normally begun. It can, therefore, be assumed that this problem was not anticipated until it was discovered just prior to the ginning season. As a result, Alphonse records storing cotton in "the hospital" and the corn crib until it could be ginned and pressed. In his journal, he complains that he has been "thrown back one month on account of [the] press."[46]

Arranging for labor was probably the biggest difficulty faced by the South after the Civil War. Both former slaves and former masters were unaccustomed to dealing with the intricacies of labor negotiations on a paid-labor basis. Additionally, former slaves were not prepared, in many cases, to determine and meet their own needs for shelter, food, clothing, and medical care, commodities formerly supplied by the planters. The Cane River planters and their former slaves probably fared better than many in other areas of the South in this regard. By the mid-1800s, the slave population of the Cane River area was largely self-reproducing, and the sale or transfer of slaves was infrequent and usually did not involve long distances.[47] Thus, the families of freed people in Louisiana may have been more intact after the Civil War than those of other regions and better able to maintain a cohesion lacking among members of the families of freed people in other states. Most former slaves in the area had roots extending back nearly as far as their former owners, with a large kinship network reaching throughout many plantations in the area.[48] This may account for the remarkably stable workforce available to the Prud'hommes in the years immediately following the Civil War.

Both during and after the Civil War, some workers did leave the plantations they had formerly served. However, people from other states moved to the area, some looking for lost relatives and others simply looking for work. New laws required that planters negotiate and sign yearly labor contracts with their

[38] This traditional family story ignores the implication that Phanor had not followed the orders of the Confederate Commander in the area to burn all stored cotton before the Federal forces could get it, which, considering his devotion to the Confederate cause, seems uncharacteristic.
[39] Breedlove, p. 36.
[40] *Ibid.*, p. 37.
[41] DeBlieux, 1993, p. 21.
[42] Lucile K. Prudhomme, "The Prud'homme Family", unpublished genealogical information on the descendants of Jean Pierre Phillipe Prud'homme, p. 3. Also see Melrose Collection, Scrapbook 256, Cammie Henry Research Center, Northwestern University, Natchitoches, Louisiana, for Phanor Prud'homme's obituary.
[43] Breedlove, pp. 56-57.
[44] *Ibid.*, p. 57.

[45] Alphonse Prud'homme, farm journal, 11 April 1866 through 12 November 1866 documents repairs to press. Series 3.1.5, folder 271, Prud'homme Collection #613, Southern Historical Collection, University of North Carolina at Chapel Hill, N.C.
[46] Prud'homme, Alphonse, n.p.
[47] Breedlove, p. 79-80.
[48] *Ibid.*, pp. 78-79.

workers. Yearly contracts began on January 4, and monthly wages ranged from $4 to $10. Nursing mothers received half pay. Working days per month ranged between 22 days and 25 days.[49] In addition, the Prud'hommes provided shelter and, apparently, some food rations as they had done for their workers prior to the Civil War. It is in the 1866 account ledgers relating to the payment of workers with newly-acquired surnames that a name first appears that is inextricably linked with the Gin Complex at Oakland Plantation: Nargot. Derzilin and Marie Nagot [sic] are listed among those who signed a yearly contract to work for the Prud'hommes in 1866.[50] They were the parents of Gabriel "Gabe" Nargot, born in October of 1867, the gin engineer most closely associated with post-bellum Oakland Plantation.

Derzilin Nagot negotiated another contract to work for the Prud'hommes for a monthly wage again in 1867, but, in 1868, the "labor arrangements began to shift somewhat" from simple paid wages to labor for a share in the crop.[51] This signaled the beginning of sharecropping as a means of contracting for agricultural labor on the Cane River plantations.

Figure 4. Prud'hommes with a bale of cotton, ca. 1905. (Photograph courtesy of Northwestern State University of Louisiana, Watson Memorial Library, Cammie G. Henry Research Center, Henley Hunter collection)

Under sharecropping arrangements, the landlord furnished the land and the seed, and the worker furnished the labor and, in some cases, equipment to raise the crop. The crop produced was then divided between the landlord and the worker according to an established method. Workers who worked "half-shares," also known as "half-hands," provided only the labor, with the landlord furnishing land, materials, and equipment for the raising of the crop. In exchange, the landlord received half of the proceeds of the crop raised by the worker. Workers who also provided equipment such as their own mules and plows to work the crop were working under a "quarter-share" arrangement. The landlord received only a quarter of the proceeds of the crop because the landlord provided only the land and seed, with the worker furnishing labor and equipment. As the Cane River planters and their workers made the transition from forced slave labor to free paid labor, overall production of cotton declined until the 1880s. Labor problems were partly to blame, but floods and caterpillars took their toll as well.[52] Year to year, production was uneven. Cotton production at Prud'hommes' plantation in1866 and 1868 was more than 100 bales, though 1867 produced only seven bales due to severe flooding in the area. In 1870, the Prud'hommes produced a total of 133 bales, but 1878 saw only twelve.[53] These figures were a far cry from the more than 600 bales produced in 1860.

After the settlement of Pierre Phanor Prud'homme's estate, the Prud'hommes' plantation was formally divided between J. Alphonse Prud'homme and Pierre Emmanuel Prud'homme in 1870. Pierre Emmanuel Prud'homme moved his family across the Cane River to his portion, which he renamed Atahoe Plantation. J. Alphonse Prud'homme renamed the portion that remained to him Oakland Plantation. Hereafter, it is the portion of the Prud'hommes' plantation that was named Oakland with which this report is concerned. Between 1883 and 1885, Robert S. Munger invented the Munger ginning system, a system still in use today. According to Britton, "Robert Munger completely reorganized the hundred-year-old tradition of plantation ginning. His concept was to automate the process, eliminating as much of the hand labor as possible...."[54] Using a pneumatic system, seed cotton was drawn out of wagons or compartments within the gin barn and conveyed to a separator mounted above the gin stands. The cotton then dropped to a conveyor belt that distributed it to feeders above each stand. Using this method, several gin stands could be linked, resulting in a series of gins to which cotton continually flowed. All the gins were connected to a common flue. The cotton that had been separated from its seeds, known as lint, was then blown through the flue to a condenser. The condenser consisted of a screen drum against which the cotton was collected, forming a batt, while dust and fine particles were blown out of the building through chimney stacks passing through the roof.

---

[49] Malone, pp. 114-115.
[50] Ibid.
[51] Ibid.

[52] Malone, p. 93.
[53] Breedlove, pp. 57-58. The figure for 1878 is for the Oakland Plantation alone.
[54] Britton, pp. 58-59.

The separated seeds were blown through another flue to a seed house for storage. The lint slid along a slanting chute from the condenser to the press.[55] This new system revolutionized and revitalized the cotton industry. For those who could afford to install a Munger system, it reduced the number of workers required at the gin to produce a bale of cotton. In concert with other innovations to the press equipment, such as the double press box, it produced bales of cotton faster. The result was that, as producing a bale of cotton became less labor-intensive, it also became less expensive and more profitable. It is probable that the Prud'hommes installed such a system by 1890.

Other labor-saving methods were introduced into the production of cotton at Oakland Plantation. According to Kenneth Prudhomme, instead of emptying the filled cotton sacks directly into a wagon that, when loaded, immediately took the cotton to the gin for processing, the cotton was dumped on a 10'x10' burlap sheet in the field. The sheet was rolled, tied, and turned over to protect it from the rain until it could be taken to the gin. Between six and eight of these bundles made up a bale of cotton, depending on how tightly they were bundled. At intervals, a wagon was driven around to the various fields, and the bundled cotton was loaded into the wagon. The wagon was compartmented, and each compartment was assigned to a worker so that the Prud'homme's could track the production of each sharecropper. When the wagon was full, the cotton was taken to the gin to be baled. Kenneth Prudhomme remembered that their wagon held enough cotton for three bales.[56] This method was less labor-intensive, as it did not require the continuous attendance of a wagon team in each field.

In addition to ginning cotton from their own plantation, the Prud'hommes provided ginning service for neighbors. "Ginning record books for the 1890s show that many area planters used the Oakland gin and that many former slaves [of the Prud'hommes' plantation] either worked for Oakland or on neighboring plantations."[57] Some of the former Prud'homme slaves who brought cotton to the Prud'hommes' gin after the Civil War were the Helaires, the Lewises, the Jean Baptistes, the Plaisances, the Edmonds, and the Honores.[58] In 1913, Edward C. Prud'homme entered a notation in his journal that is not dated, but probably was made in late November or early December, "Ginning today – yard crowded with wagons." In mid-December, he predicts a finish to ginning within a week, and notes

that "c/seed @ 12.00 here per ton, remarkably low price."[59]

Labor arrangements at the plantations along Cane River continued to fluctuate. As increased mechanization made fewer laborers necessary to the plantation owners, more of the tenant farmers were obliged to turn elsewhere for jobs. Some did not

Figure 5. Seed House, c. 1905.(Photograph courtesy of Northwestern State University of Louisiana, Watson Memorial Library, Cammie G. Henry Research Center, Henley Hunter collection)

change occupations, and many did not leave the area, but sharecropping families frequently moved to other plantations in search of better opportunities. By 1900, the sons of Derzilin Nargot, Gabe, Janvier, Severin, and Dersilin, Jr., had moved across the river to work.[60] From their positions along the river, it is possible to extrapolate for whom they were working at the time. Severin Nargot is listed in the vicinity of the Widow Cloutier's property. Janvier appears to be living on the property of Alex Cloutier. Dersilin, Jr. is located between Emmanuel and Narcisse Prud'homme, and Gabe, with a wife and two daughters, is living between the farms of Narcisse and Theophile Prud'homme.[61] Kenneth Prud'homme stated in an interview with Ann Malone that hands generally lived within walking distances of their allotted farmland. This was especially true if they were on "half-shares," which meant that they had to retrieve work animals from the landlord on a daily

---

[55] *Ibid.*, pp. 59-60.
[56] Prud'homme, Kenneth, to Ann Malone, 11 March 1997, pp. 15-16.
[57] Malone, p. 110.
[58] *Ibid.*, p. 109.

[59] *Ibid.*, p. 135.
[60] *Twelfth Census of the United States, 1900 Population Schedule, Natchitoches Parish, LA,* reviewed online at Ancestry.com, 2002, images 27-35 of 66.
[61] *Ibid.*

basis and return them at the end of the day. This observation would indicate that the Nargots were living near the lands that they farmed and near the landowners for whom they worked. Gabe Nargot's location in 1900 indicates that he may have not yet been trained to run the gin for Oakland Plantation. However, by 1910, it appears that Gabe was back at Oakland. Edward Carrington Prud'homme noted in his journal on March 27, 1910, that Gabe Nargot had not yet begun to plant his cotton, though that planted by Frank Helaire was already sprouting.[62]

Many of the descendants of former Oakland slaves were employed in one way or another at the gin and press. The Helaire family, which by 1910, had been associated with that of the Prud'hommes for 100 years, was a mainstay of the workforce. "Charley Helaire hauled wood for the gin and installed a press there. Felix Helaire worked at the press, the gin, on the bridge, drove wagons, repaired the pigeon house…"[63] However, the worker most closely associated with the gin operations at Oakland during the twentieth century was Gabe Nargot.

Ann Malone provided some background information on the Nargot family. "The Nargo family (variously spelled in the records as Argo, Nago, Nagar, Nagot, and Nargot) has…had a long association with Bermuda-Oakland. The earliest known progenitor of this family is Barbe, who was still alive on Oakland in 1870 at the age of eighty, residing in the household of her son, Dersilin (Derzilin) Nargo and his family. Her birthplace in the 1870 census is recorded as Africa, where she was born about 1790. Barrbe [sic] was probably transported to America by slavers while in her early teens for on December 7, 1809, she was nineteen and already in the possession of Emmanuel Prudhomme at Bermuda. She was among twenty-two Prudhomme slaves who were baptized in the Catholic faith at the plantation on that occasion."[64]

Gabe Nargot, grandson of Barbe, was the gin engineer for Oakland plantation in the 1920s to the early 1940s. His tenure as gin engineer doubtless ended when the gin was permanently closed in 1941 or 1942. The ruins of the cabin he occupied during this time are located in the old Quarters, southeast of the Overseer's house. The older Prud'hommes still referred to it, in 1997, as "Uncle Gabe's house,"[65] even though he had not occupied it for nearly thirty years. It was a two-room cypress and bousillage cabin with a fireplace at one end, closely resembling the tenant cabins that remain at Oakland Plantation.

Gabe Nargot is vividly remembered both by members of the Prud'homme family and by tenants who lived in the old Quarters when he lived there. Lawrence Helaire remembered him as living in the cabin alone "for a few years."[66] Carrie Helaire, daughter of Ben Helaire, who lived in the South Tenant Cabin, also remembered him as living in the cabin alone. Since her family left the area in the late 1930s, his wife had apparently died by that time.

Gabe Nargot was the gin engineer when the power for the gin was still a steam engine.[67] Phanor Prud'homme II, who inherited the plantation after his father, Alphonse, died in 1919,[68] replaced the steam engine with a diesel-burning Fairbanks Morse engine in the early to mid-twenties.[69] According to Kenneth Prudhomme, Phanor taught Gabe Nargot the intricacies of running the steam engine by keeping the boiler fired. Kenneth related a story to Ann Malone, saying that Phanor had shown Gabe repeatedly how to put his hand on the bearing to determine if the engine was becoming overheated. If the engine overheated, it was to be shut down to prevent it from exploding. As Kenneth's story goes, one day during ginning, when everything was running smoothly, Gabe unexpectedly pulled the clutch and shut everything down: the sucker pipes, the gin stand, and the press all stopped dead. Phanor ran to see what had happened. "Gabe reached over and put his hand on the cylinder of the steam engine and said, 'Mr. Phanor, that thing is hot.' Of course, [Phanor] blew up and (let loose with) a few expletives and said, 'Don't you have sense enough to know there's live steam in there? It's supposed to be hot.'"[70] Apparently, Gabe Nargot eventually learned where to place his hand to determine whether or not the engine was overheating as he remained the gin engineer for about twenty years.

The duties of the gin engineer, called the "stand man," were to maintain the gin machine, and to tend it when it was running. Kenneth Prudhomme described the gin operation of his time to Ann Malone as a three-story wooden building with a fuel-burning, diesel engine pulling the same line shaft and machinery as the old steam engine used to pull. On the bottom floor, the building held nothing but cotton storage rooms. Every hand on the plantation had his own room in which he put his cotton, and the "sucker system" was designed with an opening in every room. The hand who brought the cotton from the field ran a "sucker pipe" that sucked the cotton off

[62] Malone. p. 132.
[63] Ibid., pp. 147-148.
[64] Ibid., pp. 171-173, and 9th Census of the United States, 1870, Population Schedules, Natchitoches Parish, LA, reviewed online at Ancestry.com, 2002.
[65] Malone, pp. 171-173.

[66] Ibid., p. 190.
[67] Prud'homme, Kenneth, to Ann Malone, 11 March 1997, p. 9.
[68] Prud'homme, Lucile K., p. 4.
[69] Prud'homme, Kenneth, to Ann Malone, 11 March 1997, p. 9.
[70] Ibid., pp. 9-10.

the wagon and into the storage areas. When the hand was ready to gin his cotton, a "sucker pipe" was opened to the room that fed the cotton directly into the gin.

The main (actually, second) floor was where the gin stands and press were located. There was one fan in the gin. It sucked the cotton off the wagon, and the cotton was separated by a condenser. Then, the seed was blown to the Seed House, and the lint dropped down to be pressed. The only thing in the gin was the separator and the distributor, plus, at the top of the stand, several fans, and the press. There were more cotton storage rooms at the top of the building, on a "mezzanine" level, but they were not used in Kenneth's memory, probably because of a reduction in the labor force.[71] The system Kenneth described resembles the "Munger system," invented by Robert S. Munger in the mid-1880s and verifies that the Prud'hommes installed such a system on their plantation.

In 1940 or 1941, the cotton crop was so poor that only 7 bales of cotton were made. The gin was closed and remained idle until Alphonse, son of Phanor Prud'homme II, who was managing the plantation for his father, decided to tear it down, junk the equipment, and try to salvage what timber he could for repairs to the other farm buildings and the Main House.[72] It appears that the Gin Barn and Engine House were dismantled sometime between 1941 and 1947. The diesel engine that ran the gin equipment was sold to J.H. Williams and was at Cedar Grove plantation in 1997.[73] It is now a roadside ornament at the Cane River Gin on Highway 494 in Natchitoches. After Phanor Prud'homme closed his gin, the Prud'hommes took their cotton to Cloutier's Starlight Plantation five or six miles away for ginning.[74] Today, all that remains of the Gin Complex is the Seed House, the Cistern used to provide water to the engine when it was powered by steam, and the remains of several brick constructs designed to support the gin machinery and engine.

The Prud'hommes ceased farming operations altogether in 1985. In 1998, the National Park Service purchased 44 acres of Oakland Plantation, including the portion on which the Gin Complex stands. This acreage is now a part of the Cane River Creole National Historical Park.

---

[71] Prudhomme, Kenneth, to Ann Malone, 11 March 1997, pp. 10-12.

[72] *Ibid.*, p. 12.
[73] *Ibid.*, to Ann Malone, oral interview, 14 April 1996, transcript, p. 28.
[74] *Ibid.*, to Ann Malone, 11 March 1997, pp. 15-16.

Chronology of Development and Use

The primary components of the Gin Complex were built in 1859 through 1861. The records of Seneca Pace document the construction of what was referred to as the new gin. Construction of the new Gin Barn was completed in 1859. On January 14, 1860, the seed cotton, which was being stored in the new Gin Barn, was moved to the "mule gin," presumably for processing.[75] "On January 19th the engine at the steam [-powered] gin [complex] on the left hand bank [opposite the Main House] was dismantled and hauled across the river, a difficult and tedious job that took three days…. In August, the press on the far side [left hand bank] was dismantled and brought over to the new gin-house…"[76] The construction date of the Seed House is less certain and poorly documented. However, it seems logical to conclude that it was constructed at approximately the same time. Malone mentions two references to it recorded in January of 1861, probably in the farm journals of Seneca Pace. In one of these, the Seed House was being "covered."[77] In addition, analysis of materials and construction methods used in the Seed House indicate that the east portion of the structure dates to the 1860 construction period.

The new Gin Complex, with a Gin Barn, Seed House, Engine House, and Cistern, was located in a field south of the Overseer's House and west of the old Quarters.[78] From analysis of the materials and construction methods, it appears that the Seed House currently located there is probably at least partly the Seed House originally built at this location. About forty feet to the south of the Seed House is the location of the original Gin Barn. This estimate is based on the spacing of the supports for the seed pipe shown in the c. 1905 photograph of the Prud'hommes with a cotton bale. The Gin Barn was a three bay, three-story structure with a central gable ridge running north to south. The Seed House was connected to the Gin Barn by a 12" diameter sheet metal seed transport pipe. Approximately twenty feet south of the Gin Barn was the original location of the Engine House, which housed the steam engine and boiler. A 16'-diameter cistern about 12 feet deep was constructed between the Engine House and the Gin

Barn. The construction of the support buildings for the new Gin Barn Complex is documented in the journal of overseer Seneca Pace. On February 26, 1860, Pace recorded "Mill hands work on new gin, framing engine [house] work brick for foundation."[79] In March, he recorded that workers put the roof on the engine house, completed construction of a cistern, set the engine and worked on brick pillow for the engine shaft. Phanor Prud'homme wrote to his agent in New Orleans to arrange for insuring his new gin, estimating its value at $3000.[80] Pace's notes for April 11 and 16 "show that three men were used to construct a flue, and 390 barrels of cement were required to build the engine room's chimney (at a cost of $42.99) at the New Gin (1860 Record, 13 March, 1860, p. 12; Quarterly Inventory, p. 5; 11 April, 1860, p. 17 UNC)."[81] On July 21, 1860, three men continued to work on the new Gin Complex, laying a brick pillow for the gin stand shaft and

Figure 6. Steam engine typical of type used at Oakland Plantation.

building a ramp to the gin stand level of the Gin Barn from cypress planks.[82] During the peak of the picking season, daily yields of picked cotton were stored in the old gin complex's receiving room. (September 18, 1860 entry). On September 27, Pace recorded that the flue was finished, and the engine and pump started at the new Gin Complex. However, the pump supplying the boiler failed and had to be repaired.[83] On October 1, Pace noted that he had

---

[75] Firth, n.p., and Malone, p. 60.
[76] Firth, n.p.
[77] Malone, p. 62.
[78] The buildings of the plantation are not oriented precisely to the points of the compass. For ease of description, the orientation has been simplified. For purposes of this report, Cane River is to the east of the plantation and all buildings are oriented on that position, with north and south being assumed to be parallel to the river, east toward the river, and west away from it.

[79] Pace, n.p.
[80] Firth, n.p.
[81] Malone, pp. 60-61.
[82] Ibid., p. 61, and Firth, n.p.
[83] Firth, n.p.

ginned and pressed twenty-five bales that day. And, on November 1, he praised the performance of the gin and the new hand who was running it. With the ginning season almost over, on December 8, hands were used to fence off the new Gin Complex with split rails.[84]

The gin complexes at Oakland Plantation and at Magnolia Plantation, located just ten miles away, were contemporaries. The Oakland Gin Complex

Figure 7. Gin Barn at Magnolia Plantation.

was constructed c. 1860, and the Magnolia Gin Complex was constructed either just before or just after the Civil War. Likewise, the two ceased operation around the same time: Oakland in 1941 or 1942 and Magnolia in 1939. Based on the mid-twentieth century information on Oakland and the late nineteenth century information on Magnolia, it is known that the two gin barns had a similar capacity, each housing two gin stands. The ginning machinery at both was powered by steam in the second half of the nineteenth century and converted to diesel in the early twentieth century.

It is logical, therefore, to consider the Magnolia Gin Barn in trying to understand the layout and design of the Oakland Gin Barn. A comparison of the existing Gin Barn at Magnolia with the Oakland Gin Barn is limited by the sparse verbal and visual documentation of the Oakland Gin Barn. However, the information that does exist suggests some notable differences between the two structures. Because the Gin Barn at Magnolia Plantation still exists, and the one at Oakland Plantation does not, it is useful to compare the Magnolia Gin Barn, which we can see, with what we know of the demolished Oakland Gin Barn. For example, the construction, layout, and framing of the two are quite different. From the historic photographs and the general location of the Oakland

Gin Barn in the area between the Cistern and the Seed House, the Oakland Gin Barn appears to have been smaller in scale than the Magnolia Gin Barn. The Magnolia Gin Barn is a single bay structure with a large, steep gable roof supported by the exterior heavy timber wall framing, collar beams, and some center posts in the area of the ginning machinery and press apparatus. The photographs of the Oakland Gin Barn and the description provided by Mr. Kenneth Prudhomme indicate it had three bays: a higher central bay, which was the location of the gin stands, and two lower side bays to the west and east. The Oakland Gin Barn appears to have been more compartmentalized than the Magnolia Gin Barn and constructed to accommodate steam powered gin stands and a steam-powered press located in the center bay, with the lower east and west bays housing support functions. This supports that the Gin Barn existing in 1941 was probably the same as the one originally built c. 1860.

The presses of the two Gin Complexes were also different. The wooden screw press at Magnolia is a significant piece of craftsmanship and early technology. This appears to have been the only gin complex at Magnolia Plantation. The volume and character of the existing Magnolia Gin Barn appears to have been influenced by the need and desire to accommodate the large wooden screw press inside the barn, where all ginning took place. Oakland Plantation, on the other hand, had two to four gin barns on site over time. This may account for the construction of smaller gin buildings at Oakland Plantation than at Magnolia. Early gin complexes at Oakland Plantation possessed screw presses, both wooden and iron. When the new Gin Barn was built, the press installed in it was most likely the indoor, steam-powered, iron press purchased by Phanor Prud'homme in the 1850s.

There were differences in the orientation of the gin stands in the two gin barns. At Magnolia, the gin stands are oriented perpendicular to the long axis of the barn. With the Magnolia Engine House to the northeast of the Gin Barn, it appears there would be a drive belt of considerable length to transfer the energy from the engine to the driveline of the gin stands. The gin stand orientation and power distribution was different at Oakland. The engine, located south of the Cistern, was in close proximity to a drive shaft that extended across the Cistern and into the Gin Barn. The Gin Barn was centered over the main drive shaft. The gin stands were centered along the center axis of the three story central bay of the Oakland Gin Barn. This configuration likely produced more stress on the Oakland Gin Barn drive shaft, whereas the alignment of the engine to the driveline at Magnolia likely produced more wear and requirements for maintenance on the belt.

_____

[84] Malone, p. 62.

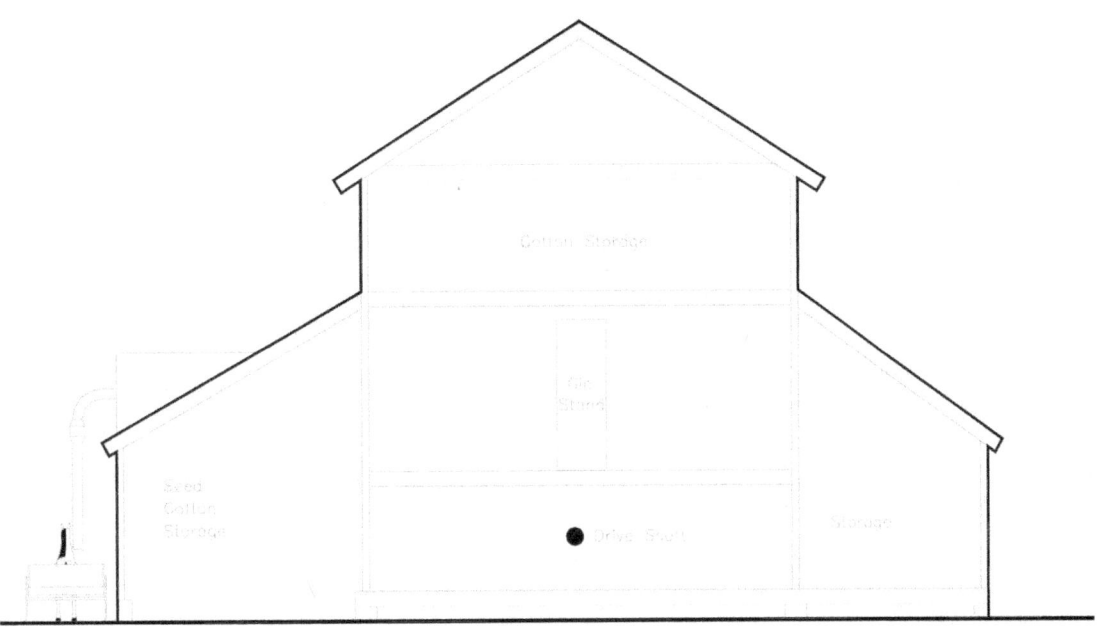

Figure 8. Interpreted east-west section of Gin Barn, facing south, based on description by Kenneth Prudhomme.

Changes to the Gin Complex after the Civil War are not well documented in the farm records and must be extrapolated from the construction and historical events. Another gin stand was ordered by Alphonse Prud'homme and delivered by the steamer *Caddo* on April 11, 1866.[85] Whether this was to replace an existing gin stand or to augment the one already in use is unknown. By 1885, Robert S. Munger had invented the Munger system of ginning. Photographs from 1905 and descriptions of the ginning operation by members of the Prud'homme family indicate that this type of system was installed at Oakland Plantation. It is probable that it was installed by 1890. Whether the original Gin Barn was removed and a new barn built to accommodate the system is unknown, but there is no evidence in plantation records that this occurred. It is probable that the Prud'hommes simply adapted their existing, c. 1860 Gin Barn to the new system.

The Munger ginning system remained in use, with some modifications to equipment and housing. In the early 1920s, the Prud'hommes replaced the steam engine with a Fairbanks Morse diesel engine on a new concrete foundation to the west of the Gin Barn.[86] This required some modification to the drive system of the gin when the mounts for the diesel engine were located to the west of the Gin Barn and

the steam engine was abandoned and the addition of a shed to house the new engine. When the diesel engine was installed, the drive shaft extending over the Cistern to the then-abandoned steam engine was cut, and a new fitting was installed to accept the drive mechanism from the diesel engine. The diesel engine was protected from the elements by a wood structure, the specific characteristics of which are unknown. The then-existing press was probably replaced at this time with the hydraulic press system recalled by Mr. Kenneth Prudhomme. Mr. Prudhomme's memory of the Gin Complex as it appeared from the early 1930s until the Gin Barn was demolished was most helpful in understanding the layout of the Gin Complex and its operation. However, it is important to note that his evidence may not be reflective of the original nineteenth century complex. The following represents information provided by Mr. Prudhomme, born in 1929, to Mr. Jack Pyburn, Historic Preservation Architect, of the Office of Jack Pyburn, Architect, Inc., on January 16, 2003, combined with information gathered from the two c. 1905 photographs and existing features of the site.

With an understanding of the overall layout of the Gin Complex and with the information provided by Mr. Prudhomme, the value of the c. 1905 photograph of the north end of the Gin Barn is amplified. From this photograph, it can be established that there was a central bay of the Gin Barn that was higher than a visible west bay. An upper eave projected over the

[85] Prud'homme, Alphonse, n.p.
[86] Prud'homme, Kenneth, to Ann Malone, 11 Mar 1997, p. 9.

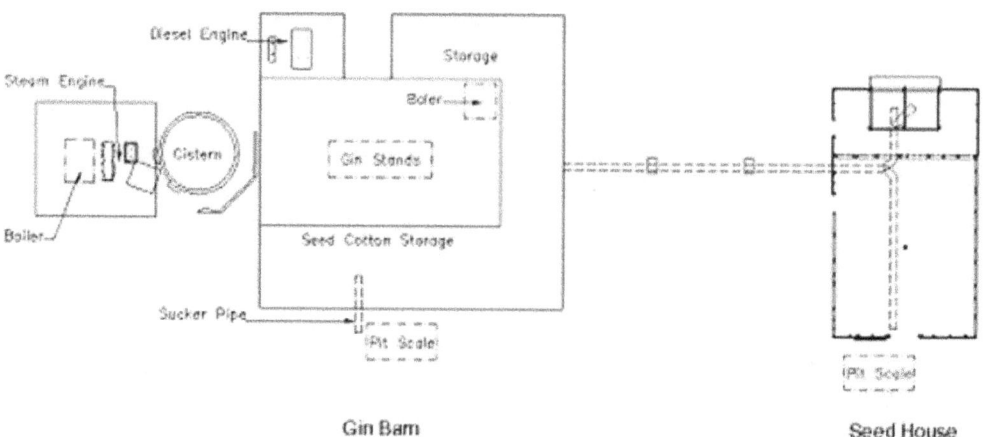

Figure 9. Interpreted plan of Gin Complex.

upper west wall of the central bay of the Gin Barn. The slope on the upper roof appears in the photograph to have been approximately a ten in twelve pitch. The rafter ends of the upper roof were likely exposed under the eave. The upper 4' to 5' of the west wall of the central bay was vertical with horizontal siding. Four to five feet below the upper center bay eave, a lower roof framed into the west (long) side of the Gin Barn. According to Mr. Prudhomme, this western bay extended from the north end of the Gin Barn to approximately the midpoint of the west elevation of the central bay. The c. 1905 photograph reveals a shed roof on the north end of the Gin Barn that framed into the vertical north wall of the center bay. The north shed area was enclosed with horizontal siding, either clapboard or horizontal planks. It is difficult to precisely determine the siding materials from the photograph. According to the photograph, the north shed area projected approximately 15' to 20' to the north from the north wall of the central bay of the Gin Barn. Mr. Prudhomme described the north end of the shed as having a roof dormer with a door where the bales were moved out of the Gin Barn and onto wagons.

Based on Mr. Prudhomme's description, the Gin Barn was symmetrical in its overall construction, with a center bay, an east bay, and a west bay. However, the projection of the east bay extended the full length of the east elevation, twice as long as the west bay. The east bay also had a dormer that accommodated the sucker pipe of the Munger system. The c. 1905 photograph shows the seed transport pipe extending from the Gin Barn, presumably to the Seed House, supported by substantial wooden posts.

The Gin Barn was constructed of wood. Based on the c. 1905 photograph, it is difficult to determine if the building was painted. However, it is known that both the Seed House at Oakland and the Gin Barn at Magnolia were not painted. Therefore, it is reasonable to assume that the Gin Barn at Oakland was also not painted.

The c. 1905 photograph suggests the north shed area had a low pier foundation. Mr. Prudhomme indicated that he remembered the larger Gin Barn structure being on piers.

Mr. Prudhomme described the interior layout of the Gin Barn as follows. The building was three stories tall. The lower floor, which was no more than two feet off the bare earth, accommodated the drive shaft and associated transfer gears and wheels for the machinery at that level and above. Mr. Prudhomme stated that some part of the lower level remained a dirt floor. However, he could not remember the specific configuration of the first level floor enough to be able to describe the extent of the dirt versus wood flooring.

According to Kenneth Prudhomme, the last press was a two box (wooden with metal straps) hydraulic up-packing baler. The foundation for the press was located on the first floor at the north end of the central bay, west of the drive shaft. Mr. Prudhomme stated that he suspected the foundation for the press was still evident at or close to the surface of the ground in the area between the Seed House and Cistern. A film of the plantation was made when the Gin Barn was still standing. This film was later converted to videotape and a copy of it is in the possession of the National Park Service. Video footage of the Gin Barn reveals a dormer on what, according to Mr. Prudhomme, appears to be the north side of the Gin Barn. This dormer contained a door. Two laborers were shown moving a bale of cotton from the Gin Barn to a wagon. With the press located in the northwest corner of the Gin Barn, the north end would be the appropriate location for loading activities to occur. This addition to the Gin Barn was probably made during the 1920s, when the steam engine was replaced with a diesel engine, and the steam-powered press was replaced, possibly, with an hydraulic one. The c. 1905 photograph of the west side of the north end of the Gin Barn provides no evidence of a dormer or loading dock for cotton bales.

The second floor of the central bay of the Gin Barn supported the separator, two gin stands, a fan, and a condenser. The second floor of the east bay housed seed cotton storage bins for the tenants and, later, for local community farmers who were also serviced during the years of ginning operations at Oakland. The sucker pipe that moved seed cotton from wagons to both the bins and Gin Barn was located on the east side of the east bay in a dormer on the low roof. The west bay of the second floor probably housed the rest of the up-packing press machinery, and would have been the location of the bale-loading activities.

Mr. Prudhomme did not recall the use of the third floor, but historical research suggests the third floor was once used for seed cotton storage, though that practice had been discontinued by the 1930s. Based on the c. 1905 photograph, the third floor was likely confined to the central bay.

The shorter west wing of the Gin Barn housed spare parts and "junk" from around the site. Mr. Prudhomme stated children were not allowed in the west bay because it was so disorganized and dangerous.

It is not possible, based on currrent information, to determine how many of the outside bay additions were modifications to an earlier configuration of the Oakland Gin Barn. However, it is likely that some of the sheds located off the central bay were added. It is known that the east bay at the Oakland Gin Barn accommodated storage bins for tenant and community farmers in its later years of operation. The east bay extended the full length of the central bay in the north-south direction. The sucker pipe was in a dormer over the east bay. The low-pitched shed on the north side of the Oakland Gin Barn in the c.1905 photograph appears to be an addition to the central, three-story structure. There are no known photographs of the west elevation. Kenneth Prudhomme remembered that there was a room off the central bay to the west that extended from the northwest corner of the central bay to approximately

Figure 10. Photo, c. 1905, showing part of the gin barn and the seed-transport pipe.

the middle of the west elevation of the central bay. This configuration could well have been an addition. The Engine House constructed for the diesel engine installed in the 1920s on the south end of the western elevation of the central bay is a known addition. In contrast to the Magnolia Gin Barn, which was simpler in its exterior configuration and spacious enough to accommodate modifications in the ginning process on its interior, the Oakland Gin Barn was smaller and likely accommodated changes in the ginning process and operations with additions.

At some point, the pit scale initially located on the east side of the Seed House was moved to the east side of the Gin Barn. The weighing mechanism was also relocated from the Seed House to the second floor of the Gin Barn to be run by the sucker pipe operator.

Unlike the Gin Barn, the Seed House still exists and can provide some clues regarding its history. Framing of the Seed House indicates that it was enlarged to the west at some time after it was originally constructed. The earliest documentation of the Seed House is a photograph with the structure in the background. This photograph was likely taken on the same day as the c. 1905 Gin Barn photograph, based on evidence of the clothing worn by the people in the photograph. Several characteristics of the Seed House are notable in the c. 1905 photograph. In the photograph, there is no shed roof on the south side of the structure. There is what appears to be a gutter system with a drainage trough extending toward the Gin Barn and, possibly, the Cistern. However, the existing Cistern seems to be too far from the Seed House to expect water to be collected from the Seed House roof, particularly given the amount of ginning

Figure 11. Seed house. c. 1999.

activity (weighing and sucking cotton) known to be taking place on the east side of the Gin Barn. The east shed roof is visible in the c. 1905 photograph. Two metal vent stacks are visible, one on each gable end of the original structure. The south windows are not visible, but they could have been covered by their shutters and, thus, not visible in the photograph, given the distance the photographer was from the Seed House.

An examination of the 1941 aerial photograph reveals that the east shed of the Seed House was deeper than the current shed. The depth of the east shed in this photograph would probably require post supports. The 1941 shed configuration would have been able to accommodate a wagon and may have been of the period when the pit scales were located at the east end of the Seed House. There is a suggestion in the 1941 aerial photograph that both the south shed and the seed transfer pipe were in place at that time. The configuration of the south shed and the alignment of the seed transfer pipe are consistent in both the 1941 aerial photograph of the site and the c. 1905 photograph of the Gin Barn.

Ginning was conducted in the following manner. Upon arrival, a wagon would pull up to the east side of the Gin Barn to have the seed cotton removed from the wagon using the sucker pipe. The cotton would either be processed through the gin stands at that time or stored in a designated bin in the west bay of the Gin Barn. Once processed, the ginned cotton went to the press on the north end of the Gin Barn and the seed went to the Seed House via the metal Munger transport pipe. If the seed was collected for a customer, it was diverted to one of two chutes on the west end of the Seed House. If the seed was collected for plantation use, it was diverted to the floor of the Seed House. After completion of the ginning process, a customer could pull up to the west end of the Seed House and load the seed into his wagon via the seed chute. He could then pull his wagon around to the north side of the Gin Barn and

have his cotton loaded before exiting the site.

The Prud'hommes stopped ginning their own cotton in 1941 or 1942. Thereafter, the buildings fell into disuse and, ultimately, disrepair. Eventually, the Prud'hommes dismantled the Gin Barn and Engine House. A 1941 aerial photograph of the site shows the Gin Complex buildings intact. Maps of the plantation drawn from a 1947 aerial photograph and a 1958 aerial photograph reference the "site of gin building," and the "site of boiler room," though other buildings and structures on the property are referenced simply by their name. Therefore, it is reasonable to assume that both the boiler room and Gin Barn were no longer in existence when the 1947 aerial photograph was taken. The Seed House, the Cistern, and the brick supports for gin and engine equipment alone remain to bear witness to the location of the Gin Complex.

The National Park Service purchased 44 acres of Oakland Plantation in 1998 to incorporate into the proposed new Cane River Creole National Historical Park. The Gin Complex was part of this purchase. By the time the National Park Service acquired the plantation in 1994, the Seed House had shed roofs on both the north and south elevations of the main structure. A c. 1999 photograph reveals the clapboard siding on the east elevation and the exposed framing on the south elevation. The historic east door is visible, and the metal roof is also visible. The Park's staff reports that the structure's foundation, which was substantially wood, was in an advanced state of deterioration. In 1999, the National Park Service completed stabilization and preservation treatments at the Seed House.

Summary of National Park Service Treatments

Stabilization and rehabilitation of the Seed House to adapt it for facility management functions were undertaken in 1999 by the National Park Service to respond to direction regarding use and treatment established in the National Park Service General Management Plan (GMP) for the Cane River Creole National Historical Park. Though in an advanced stage of structural failure, a significant amount of the historic features of the structure were existing at the time the National Park Service acquired the site. These included: floor beams, the wood frame superstructure, the roof framing for the east portion of the building, the seed hopper, a meaningful amount of exterior and interior siding, window framing, corrugated and 5V-profile metal roofing, and the west seed chute shutters. Based on the Design Analysis prepared by the Cane River Creole

National Historical Park staff dated September 25, 2001 and on field observations, the rehabilitation and adaptive use work by the National Park Service since 1999 has included:

Constructing new foundation piers of brick and cinder block. These piers replace what were historic wood piers on stone pads that were structurally unsuitable for reuse. Non-historic materials and methods were used for the new foundation.

Repair and replacement of floor framing. The floor joists in the east portion of the structure were sistered with contemporary 2" by 10" lumber. The floor joists and south sill beam were replaced in the west seed chute addition.

Replacement of flooring with plywood. The original flooring in the Seed House was 4/4"[87] by 12" butt-jointed planks deemed by the National Park Service staff to be sufficiently deteriorated to require replacement. To accommodate the light carpentry use for which the building is slated under its facility management designation, the decision was made to use ¾" plywood sub-flooring and finish flooring. At the time of the site visit for this report, the sub-flooring was in place. It was reported by staff at the site that the finish layer of flooring is to be ¾" plywood cut into 12" widths and installed in a butt-jointed fashion.

Reinstallation of existing metal roofing and replacement of deteriorated roofing. The roofing on the main structure (both east and west sections) was numbered, removed, and replaced in its original location with new fasteners, as was the metal roofing on the east and north shed roofs. The south and west sheds have received new roofing to match the characteristics of the deteriorated metal roofing found on the structure at the outset of stabilization. To accommodate the proposed use and occupancy of the Seed House, the roof assembly was modified from the historic assembly. The historic assembly included rafter framing with lath boards as sheathing and metal roofing panels attached to the lath. The adapted roof assembly includes the historic rafters and lath, the addition of building felt, 1½" insulation board, and an adhesive backed membrane moisture barrier, all covered by the historic metal roofing panels.

Stabilization and reinforcing of the structural framing. The existing structural framing that was judged by National Park Service staff to be sound was retained and re-secured.

Figure 12. Seed House, east elevation.

Figure 13. Seed House, north elevation.

Reconstruction and modification of exterior walls. One of the most significant modifications to the original assembly of the Seed House has been the adaptation of the historic wall system to accommodate conditioned space. While the building is not planned to be air conditioned, it will be heated and insulated for occupant comfort. In addition to the modification of the roof assembly, the wall assemblies were altered to retain the historic exterior presentation and produce an interior finish with the same materials as on the original north and south elevations. The north and east elevation siding appears to be mostly historic with some new materials added to replace materials that had substantially deteriorated. The west elevation siding was reconstructed to match the historic siding in dimensions and species. On the north and south elevations and in between the interior and exterior finishes, a layer of insulation and a vapor barrier were installed. To accommodate the additional wall thickness, furring strips were attached on the inside of hewn columns. On the east and west interior elevations, the hewn, heavy timber wall framing was left exposed. Behind the historic east elevation exterior siding and the west elevation siding is a layer of insulation with an interior finish of Homosote, a proprietary fiberboard with sound and temperature

---

[87] The use of fractions in lumber dimensions denotes true measurements. For example, 4/4 indicates four quarters of an inch or a 1" lumber dimension.

insulating qualities. This finish is installed between the heavy timber framing members.

Framing for the bathroom and utility closet in the northwest corner of the building included installing conventional stud walls and gypsum wallboard. The bathroom and utility closet extend to the height of the original upper plate, substantially retaining visibility of the overall volumetric qualities of the interior of the Seed House. The primary impact of the bathroom, which encloses the northwest corner of the west addition, is on the character and understanding of the historic seed chute.

Reframing of the north and south shed roofs with additional diagonal supports. As can be seen in the c. 1999 photograph, the south shed framing had failed. It was determined by National Park Service staff that the structural framing of the north and south sheds was inadequate. Supplemental framing was installed on both shed roofs prior to the installation of roofing panels.

Construction and installation of exterior doors with reinforced plywood exterior doors. When the National Park Service acquired Oakland Plantation, only the east horizontal sliding door of the Seed House was extant. The original door openings were retained, and non-historic plywood doors were fabricated and installed. The Design Analysis for the rehabilitation and adaptive use of the structure states that the temporary doors will be replaced with 1¾" vertical rough-sawn cypress plank doors with interior horizontal battens.

The investigation of 2002 conducted for this Historic Structure Report revealed that interior modifications to the Seed House are proceeding. Temporary electrical service has been installed and, it is presumed, water and sanitary utilities will be installed soon.

Figure 14. NPS rehabilitative work on the floor framing system of the Seed House, 1999. Note sistering of historically sloped floor beams to achieve level floor surface.

Physical Description

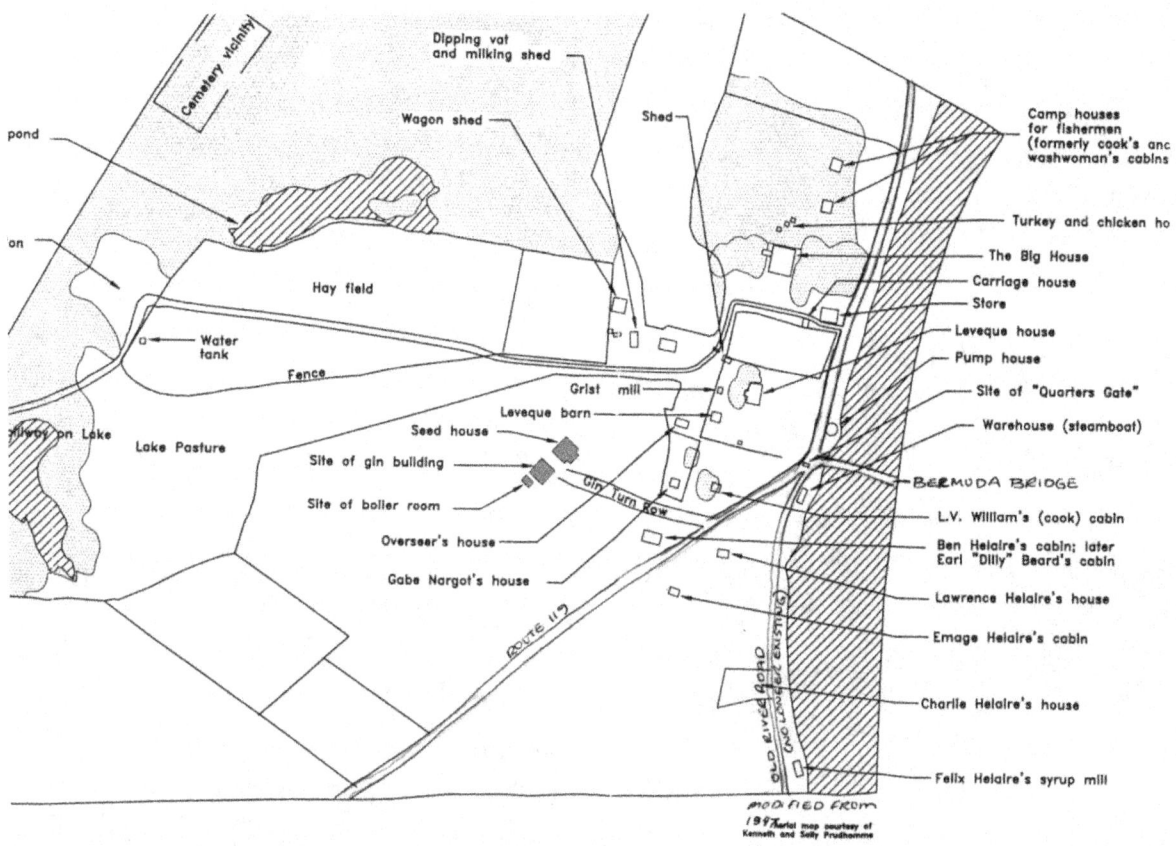

Figure 15. Drawing from 1947 aerial photo of Oakland Plantation with Gin Complex indicated by dark shading.

The existing Seed House, Cistern, and engine foundations located southwest of the Overseer's House are surviving features of a Gin Complex, the primary components of which were built in 1859 and 1860.[88] The Gin Complex, of which the existing Seed House is part, is known to have included a Gin Barn, the existing Seed House, a steam engine and Engine House, a diesel engine and Engine House, a Cistern, and two pit scales.

Based on the c. 1941 photograph of the layout and an understanding of the operation of the Gin Complex, a number of features have been lost, with no visible evidence as to their precise location. They include the

Gin Barn structure, the Steam Engine Boiler, the Press Foundation, the Pit Scales at the east elevation of the Seed House, and the Pit Scales at the east elevation of the Gin Barn

The locations of the Steam Engine House and Diesel Engine House are known from the remains of the support structures for the engines they housed, but the extents of their footprints is unknown.

The historic Gin Complex site includes the Seed House, the Cistern, two masonry foundations south of the Cistern, and two concrete foundations northwest of the Cistern. The two masonry foundations south of the Cistern supported the steam engine, the first power source for the gin stands and press. South of the masonry engine mounts was the brick-enclosed boiler. The machinery was located in its own structure, called the Engine House in plantation records. In the 1920s, the steam engine and boiler were replaced by a Fairbanks Morris diesel engine

---

[88] The buildings of the plantation are not oriented precisely to the points of the compass. However, for ease of description, the orientation has been simplified. For purposes of this report, Cane River is to the east of the plantation and all buildings are oriented on that position, with north and south being assumed to be parallel to the river, east toward the river, and west away from it.

Figure 16. Cistern with cover.

Figure 17. Steam engine foundation mount.

Figure 18. Fairbanks-Morse engine from Oakland Plantation.

located to the west of the Gin Barn. The foundations for this engine are those to the northwest of the existing cistern. This section of the Historic Structure report contains descriptions of the remaining features of the historic Gin Complex. Descriptions of missing features may be found in the Chronology of Development and Use section of this report.

Cistern

The Cistern is located about 240' south of the Seed House. Constructed of brick, it measures 15'-3" in diameter and 12'-2½" deep. This volume produced a capacity of 13,553 gallons of water when full. Mechanical engineers at Hartrampf, Inc. calculated that, when full, the Cistern could provide about 400 hours, or about 17 days, of operation of the steam engine before it would require replenishing. The masonry wall of the Cistern is 9" thick and coated with plaster on the interior. The plaster is in fair condition. The exterior wall has remnants of a stucco coating.

A wood-framed cover was installed on the top of the Cistern during the stabilization phase of work at Oakland. The cover is fitted with screen wire on the underside as a safety measure and to discourage both mosquito breeding and debris collection.
What appears to be a brick wall at grade is located just northeast of the Cistern. This wall is possible evidence of a larger brick structure built at this location. The portion of the wall exposed at grade appears to share a common center point with the extant Cistern and could indicate the presence of an earlier, larger cistern at this location. However, no information has been found to provide any additional insight into the character or purpose of this structural remnant.

Visual observation suggests that the Cistern is, overall, structurally sound but not without problems. Several cracks in the brick wall were observed. The condition of the Cistern is considered to be fair to poor given the weakened condition and substantial delamination and loss of the stucco coating on the interior and exterior walls and the evidence of cracking on the interior wall.

Steam Engine Foundations

The steam engine equipment foundations are located on the south side of the Cistern and are constructed of masonry with embedded threaded rods used to anchor the engine to its foundation. The condition of the south equipment mounts is poor. The masonry is deteriorated, and a significant number of the bricks are missing. The feature is exposed to the elements. According to Mr. Kenneth Prudhomme, the steam engine was mounted to these foundations and housed in a structure, the Engine House, for weather protection. The boiler was located immediately south of the steam engine and was encased in brick. Mr. Prudhomme recalled that, when the boiler was dismantled in the 1920s, the brick from the boiler housing was used for other purposes on the plantation, most notably, the construction of the east and south steps to the Main House.

Diesel Engine Foundations

The Fairbanks Morse engine from the Oakland Gin Complex is now a roadside ornament at the Cane River Gin on Highway 494 in Natchitoches. The remaining evidence of the diesel engine and its associated components is two concrete foundations with threaded rods extending from the top for anchorage of the engine. The two foundations are of different sizes. The north foundation is 4'-3" by 8'-0" and is 1'-3" above grade. The north foundation has four 1" threaded rods extending 8" above the top of the foundation. The foundation concrete contains brick chards as aggregate, similar to the material used on the porch supports of the South Tenant Cabin and found in some concrete pieces in the vicinity of the Main House. The south foundation is smaller, 1'-4" by 5'-0" and is 2'-0" above the prevailing grade. It is constructed of the same concrete composition as the north foundation. The two ¾"-diameter threaded rods on the center axis of this foundation extend approximately 3" above the top of the concrete and sit in 3" steel sleeves. The south foundation is 3'-3" south of the north foundation. The west equipment mounts are in fair condition. They appear to be structurally stable but are chipped. The threaded steel rods are exposed to the elements and are continuing to rust and deteriorate.

Seed House

The Seed House is a one-story wood frame structure set on piers and measuring 50'-7" by 30'-2", approximately 2,550 square feet of enclosed space. The structure has been modified at least once since construction. The larger, eastern portion of the building measures 37'-7" by 30'-2". The western portion was an addition, and measures 30'-2" by 13'-0". Each elevation of the building has a shed roof attachment. The Seed House is rectangular in plan, with a gable roof running east to west. The structure has six windows, four on the north elevation and two on the south elevation. There are three door openings on the exterior of the building, two on the south elevation and one on the east elevation. The west elevation contains shutters at the seed chute. On the interior, the structure is an open room except for the newly-constructed unisex restroom in the northwest corner and the storage room immediately east of the

Figure 19. Machine mountings southwest of Seed House.

restroom. A line of five columns at the west end of the east section of the building and east of the seed chute on the west wall of the structure indicate the likely western extent of the original Seed House.

An understanding of the characteristics and function of the Seed House have been enhanced with the assistance of gin historian, Mr. Tommy Brown of Continental Eagle Corporation, of Prattville, Alabama, and the description of the Oakland Seed House provided by Mr. Kenneth Prudhomme. In his description of the overall layout and operation of the Gin Complex, Mr. Prudhomme stated that the pipe in the c. 1905 photograph of the Gin Barn connected to the Seed House at the location of the still-existing galvanized nipple. On the interior of the Seed House, the galvanized fitting converted to a square wooden pipe running to approximately the middle of the Seed House. There, a tee valve fitting allowed the blown seed to be routed either to one of the two seed chutes on the west end of the building or to the main floor of the Seed House on the east end of the building. If diverted to the seed chutes, there was another valve that directed the seed to either of the two chutes. The arm and lever for this valve exists under the south seed chute. The floor of the Seed House is sloped from the middle of the building to the north and south. Both Mr. Prudhomme and Mr. Brown thought the sloped floor was to assist in obtaining a reasonable distribution of the seed in the main room of the Seed House. Mr. Prudhomme stated that the windows on the north and south sides of the building never had screens or sashes. They were for controlling dust, providing light, and, at times, shoveling seed into wagons from the side of the house. This would mean that, for moving plantation seed, wagons pulled up to either the north or south side of the Seed House to be filled with seed from the windows. Mr. Prudhomme stated that, at one time, the pit scale used to weigh wagonloads of cotton was at the east end of the Seed House, set in the ground with the weighing apparatus located inside the Seed House. The scale was later moved to the Gin Barn and was in that location at the time the barn was demolished.

When considering the age of the Seed House, the characteristics of the wood and the nails used in the structure were evaluated in conjunction with the historical information in this report. The larger, eastern part of the structure is hewn post and beam construction. The joints at the columns with the sill and top wall plates are of mortise-and-tenon construction. In the eastern part of the structure, wood pegs at the heavy timber joints were not found.

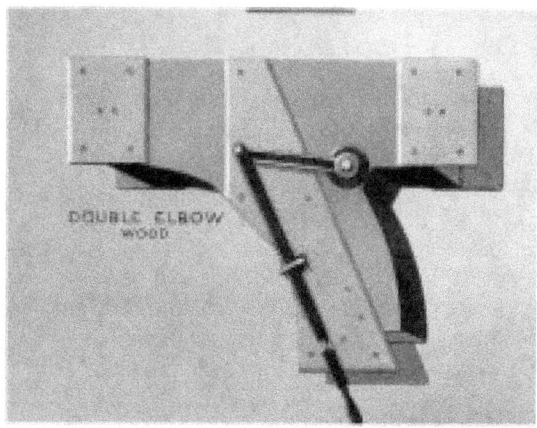

Figure 20. Valve at west chute, Munger Corporation Catalog, 1899.

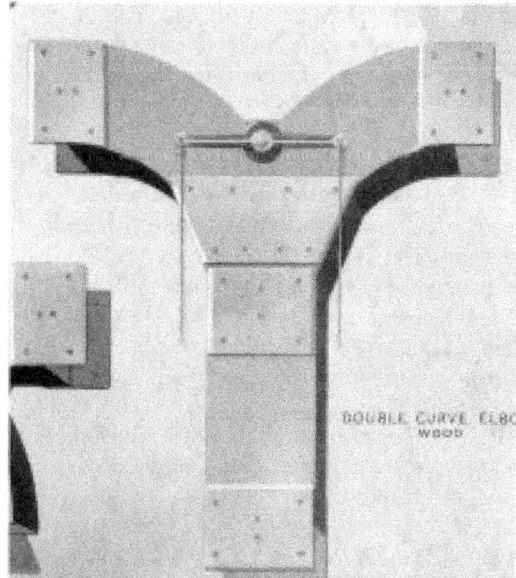

Figure 21. Seed-handling valve, Munger Corporation Catalog, 1899.

Instead, wrought iron spikes were observed to secure the joint. The roof structure was circular sawn and nailed with wire nails. The historic roof sheathing was circular sawn, as well. Based on this information and the knowledge of the manual operation of the Seed House in loading seed from the north and south windows, it is believed that the eastern portion of the Seed House dates to the 1860 period of construction of the Gin Complex.

The western 13' addition to the Seed House is all circular sawn wood structure and finish material. The connections use wire nails. The c. 1905 photograph of both the Gin Barn with seed pipe and the Seed House confirm that the Munger cotton processing system was installed at that time. The c. 1905 photograph of the Seed House shows two vent stacks at the gable, one on each gable end of the main (east) portion of the building. In this photograph, the western part of the Seed House, which currently contains the chute, does not appear to be in place. This suggests that the Munger system was installed in the east portion of the building prior to the construction of the west addition and likely after the Seed House had been in operation for seed management using manpower to move seed into and out of the structure. This would place the installation of the Munger system sometime after 1885 when the system was developed and marketed and before 1905, the date of the historic photograph. The west chute addition would then have been constructed after 1905. It seems likely that the construction of the west seed chute addition related either to the point in time when the Prud'hommes began or expanded ginning services to area farmers or to the installation of new equipment after the ginning operations were converted from steam to diesel power.

Foundation Piers

Historically, the perimeter piers of the Seed House were brick and wood. When the National Park Service acquired the property, the piers were in an advanced state of deterioration. New brick piers on reinforced concrete footings were constructed in 1999.

The interior piers were historically wooden piers on stone pads as well as brick piers. Wooden piers were beneath the floor joists, and brick piers were beneath the central and western sill beams. The wooden piers had deteriorated by the time the National Park Service acquired the property. These interior piers were replaced with new brick piers on concrete foundations under the center girder beam in the east portion of the structure and under the north heavy timber framed sill. Where historic stone foundations remained, they were retained, and new concrete masonry unit (CMU) piers were installed on them. Where no stone foundation pads remained and where

supplemental foundation support was deemed
necessary by the Park Service staff, new concrete
cinder pads and CMU piers were installed. All Seed
House piers were fitted with galvanized caps for
termite control by National Park Service staff.
The layout of the historic piers relates to the
evolution of the structure. The Seed House was
constructed in two phases. The eastern, and oldest,
part of the building, measuring approximately 30' by
36', is constructed with an intermediate line of piers
in the east-west direction 17'-4" from the north wall
of the building. As a part of the National Park
Service stabilization work, supplemental CMU piers
on cinder block pads were installed at the mid-span
of the south 8" by 8" floor joists. It is interesting to
note that, historically, there was no pier under the
center column of the eastern portion of the Seed
House. The column rested on a 12" by 12" beam.
This configuration has been retained in the recent
National Park Service stabilization and rehabilitation
work.

The foundations for the west portion of the Seed
House, constructed later than the east portion, include
perimeter piers that have been reconstructed by Park
Service staff with new brick on reinforced concrete
foundations. There is no evidence that the support
columns for the seed chute originally had any piers
under them. This would have caused the bulk of the
weight from the seed to be supported at mid-span of
14' beams, creating a likely condition for deflection,
if not structural failure. A line of supplemental piers
was installed by Park Service staff at approximately
mid-span of the 14' wide structure. The
supplemental piers are parged brick on concrete
footings.

Structural System
Floor Framing: The floor framing is different in each
of the two sections of the Seed House. The
components of the eastern part of the structure
include 12" by 12" perimeter sill beams. Where
sound, historic beams were retained in the
stabilization and rehabilitation of the structure.
However, the perimeter sill beams were replaced by
Park Service staff the full length of the south side of
the east structure. The east-most span of the north
beam line and the south-most span of the west beam
line were also replaced. These beams were replaced
to match the dimensions of the historic beams.
The interior framing of the eastern part of the Seed
House is quite interesting. The interior framing
layout is asymmetrical in plan and elevation. The
interior floor beam runs east and west and is 17'-4"
from the north beam line. The resulting south span of
the floor system is 12'-10". The north span has a
slope of 5½" of fall from the interior beam to the
north wall and a slope of 1½" of fall from the interior
beam to the south wall. Clues that this was an

Figure 22. Seed House, south elevation.

Figure 23. Seed House, west elevation.

Figure 24. Typical perimeter Pier/ Post 1999.

intentional detail of the building are that the building
eaves are at the same elevation above grade, and the
characteristics of the interior east/west beam
accommodate the slope. Both Tommy Brown,
Continental Eagle historian, and Mr. Kenneth
Prudhomme thought that the slope was intended to
assist in distributing seed across the floor of the
building.
Historic floor joists in the eastern part of the Seed
House are 8" by 8" and 10" by 10" hewn members
set at varying spacing but, on average, about 4' on
center. The flooring of the Seed House originally

spanned from hewn joist to hewn joist. As a part of the National Park Service stabilization and rehabilitation of the structure, pressure treated 2" by 10" members were sistered on both sides of each original hewn member with lag screws. Supplemental 2" by 10" members were installed between the hewn floor joists using galvanized joist hangers to achieve a span of approximately 16" on center. Two by ten inch spacers were also installed at the third points between each new joist.

The floor framing of the west 14' addition originally consisted of three 8" by 8" hewn beams at quarter points, with 7'-6" spans. The floor framing of the west addition was significantly altered in the National

Figure 25. Interior framing of east wall.

Park Service rehabilitation efforts. Supplemental 2" by 10" floor joists were installed at equal spans running east and west with the sawn joists to reduce the unsupported length of the flooring above. The new joists served also to level the flooring. Two by ten inch spacers were also installed at the third points of the span. Modification of the floor framing was designed to address deterioration of the existing historic framing members and the inadequacy of the historic framing pattern to accommodate desired loads on the floor above. However, to the extent possible, historic framing members, particularly floor beams, were retained. If the deterioration was such that they could not be retained, they were replaced in-kind. The primary modification by the Park Service staff to the floor framing was the addition of intermediate joists to reduce the inordinately long spans for floorboards above.

To evaluate the structural capacity of the floor framing system, the Seed House floor system was modeled in *Visual Analysis 5.0* using structural elements defined by field observations and drawings from the National Park Service. The National Park Service has already performed rehabilitation of the Seed House, and most of the framing is comprised of

new members, so evaluation was based on the existing, "repaired" condition. A structural analysis was performed on the floor system and checked for compliance with the 2000 International Building Code (IBC) based on flexure, shear, and deflection criteria. The General Management Plan for the Park designates the Seed House to "accommodate the park's primary indoor maintenance functions."[89] Conversations with Park personnel indicate that this is interpreted to mean that the Seed House will be used as an office and assembly area for maintenance personnel, though some carpentry equipment, such as the table saw that is currently in the Seed House, could remain in use. Since the Seed House will be used as an office, a minimum live load of 60 psf, was applied to the floor system. This is the load required by the International Building Code for office spaces. A dead load of 10 psf in addition to the actual member weights was also applied to the floor system. The results of this analysis show that in its existing configuration many framing members are not adequate for the intended use as required by current building codes.

Discussions with on-site National Park Service staff at Oakland Plantation indicate that there are plans to add another layer of plywood sheathing to the floor. If this additional layer is added, the Seed House floor and its supporting members will be adequate for a live load of 60 psf, but not for an assembly load of 100 psf. The additional flooring must have a minimum thickness of ¾ inch and be securely fastened to the floor joists using minimum 10d common nails spaced no more than 16" on center. For the Seed House to function as office space per the Park's General Management Plan without strengthening the floor framing system underneath, this additional plywood sheathing must be added to the floor.

The Seed House was originally constructed using methods and materials typical for the period. The National Park Service made repairs to the facility based on the dimensions of the original construction. National Park Service personnel recognized some of the deficiencies of the original design with regard to the intended use of the structure by the Park and attempted to remedy them by installing supplementary framing. The minimum live load required for the intended use of the structure as an office is 60 psf. This is one and one-half times the amount allowed by the original framing methods. Additionally, the Phase II designation for this building is as an educational facility. What type of educational facility the Park intends to put in the

[89] National Park Service, *Cane River Creole National Historical Park Draft General Management Plan/Environmental Impact Statement*, Denver: U.S. Department of the Interior, 2001, p. 15.

Seed House is not determined. The floor framing members do not meet the standard of providing 100 psf load required for assembly areas by current building codes. However, it does meet the current building code requirements of 40 psf for classrooms. Classrooms include students, desks, and chairs. Use of the Seed House for a classroom would not require any strengthening of the floor framing system to meet current building codes.

Wall Framing: Like the foundations and floor framing, the wall framing differs in the eastern part of the Seed House from that in the western addition. The wall framing and top plate of the eastern section are hewn members. Field observations indicate some hewn members were reused. This is most notable on the top plate of the west wall framing of the eastern section, which show open, unused mortises. The wall framing on the north and south side of the eastern section of the Seed House is exposed on the exterior. The east wall framing is exposed on the interior. The framing of what was the west exterior wall before the expansion of the building is now an line of interior columns. The wall framing members on the east wall of the Seed House vary from 6" by 8" to 5" by 6". There are four hewn posts to the north and south of the east door. The posts are connected to the sill and top plate by mortise and tenon joints. However, no wood pegs were observed. Instead, forged spikes were used to secure the joints.

The wall framing on the south wall of the east section of the building is similar to that of the east wall except that it is exposed to the exterior from the east corner to the east jamb of Door 101. The spacing of the posts varies from 4'-8" to 5'-10". Post sizes vary from 9" by 7" at the east corner to 3" by 5¼" at the east door jamb. West of Door 101 on the south side of the east section, the hewn wall framing posts are again on the interior. There are three posts between the west jamb of Door 101 and the southwest corner of the east section of the building.

The west framing columns of the east section were, prior to the construction of the west addition, part of an exterior wall. Including the corner posts, there are seven posts in this column line. As on the other three sides of the east part of the building, the size of the posts varies considerably. This variation is a strong indication that the eastern part of the Seed House was constructed with some reused materials. This conjecture is further supported by the vacant mortises on the topside of the top plate of the framing in this column line. The vertical support above the top plate to the ridge is a hewn member, as is the corresponding ridge support on the east wall. The wall framing for the entire north wall of the east section of the building is exposed to the exterior. Its characteristics are similar to the other three walls of

the east section. Posts on the eastern section of the building vary from 4" by 3" to 6" by 3". Spacing of the posts is random and varies between 2'-6" and 4'-6".

Figure 26. Detail of roof framing.

The western 14' addition is uniform in the characteristics of its framing members. The framing members of the addition are all circular sawn, true-dimension lumber. The historic single 2" by 4" roof framing was deteriorated by the time the National Park Service acquired the property. When it was reconstructed by the Park Service in recent stabilization and rehabilitation activities it was determined that the single 2" by 4" members were structurally inadequate. Therefore, the roof framing was changed to two 2" by 4" joists in place of the single joists.

Structurally, the wall framing and connections appear to be adequate for the intended use of the building. No further modifications to the wall framing are required to provide normal structural strength and stability.

Roof Framing: The roof framing of the eastern portion of the building is 2" by 6" circular-sawn rafters at approximately 30" on center. The framing extends from the north and south walls to a ridge beam composed of three 2" by 6" boards stacked in their short dimension. The roof framing on the western portion of the building is 2" by 4" true-dimension rafters. The unsupported span of the ridge beam is reduced by bracing the interior column in the eastern section of the building. The bracing is an assembly of two 2" by 6" and one 1½" by 6" sawn members. These members appear to be straight sawn, with an angled pit-sawn saw mark characteristic. However, these saw marks are not found elsewhere in the building. This suggests that these members, like many others, if not most, in the

Figure 27. Door 100
Note sliding door adjacent to opening.

building were reused from other earlier structures. Supporting the rafters at midpoints of every other roof rafter are 2½" by 5" hand- hewn collar beams.

The roof sheathing is extant 4/4" by 12" boards and new 4/4" by 12" cypress sheathing boards that replaced deteriorated historic boards deemed structurally inadequate by the Park Service staff. The roof sheathing is laid with a 1" to 2" gap supporting building felt, insulation board, and the metal panel roofing above. The sheathing is in its historic location.

The structure of the south shed roof was reconstructed by the National Park Service staff using new, rough-sawn cypress cross ties and pressure treated 2" by 4" rafters. New ¾" by 12" sheathing boards were installed to support the metal panel roofing.

The entire structure for the west shed over the seed chute was reconstructed by the National Park Service staff in the stabilization phase of improvements. To address an inherent structural deficiency in the historic framing, three diagonal braces were also installed to supplement the original framing configuration.

The existing east shed roof structure was repaired, and the historic metal roofing panels were reinstalled by National Park Service staff.

Roofing Assembly: The historic roofing assembly included metal roofing panels on 4/4" sheathing. The stabilization and rehabilitation work performed by the National Park Service on the main roof, both the east and the west sections, modified that historic assembly by adding a layer of roofing felt on top of the sheathing, a 1½" layer of rigid insulation, a second layer of 30# roofing felt, and a layer of waterproofing membrane underlayment (Ice and Water Shield) between the sheathing and the historic metal panels. This assembly modification was made to facilitate the adaptive use of the building for

facility management. The roofing material on the main building is a mixture 1½" corrugated and 5V profile metal panels.

The north shed roofing is historic 2" corrugated metal panels on the extant structure. On the south shed, new 2" corrugated roofing has been installed, as the old roofing materials on this shed had been lost. New 5V-profile metal panels have been installed on the west shed. The east shed was reconstructed using existing 5V-profile metal roofing.

Structurally, the existing roof assembly is in excellent condition. The metal panels are in good condition. No further modifications are required to the roof assembly to provide normal structural strength and stability.

Doors

At the time the National Park Service acquired the property, only the eastern 8' long horizontal sliding door existed. This door has now been fixed in place on the remains of its steel track hardware by Park Service staff. All door openings in the Seed House are in their historic locations. At the time of this report, all door openings had been fitted with temporary, unfinished ¾" plywood doors with 1" by 4" nominal bracing, except for the doors on the east facade, which have 1" by 6" nominal bracing. The Design Analysis for the Seed House indicates that permanent exterior doors will be made of 1¾" cypress planks with horizontal back battens. Interior doors are planned to be of similar character but of planed-finish yellow pine.

The hardware on the temporary doors consists of modern, galvanized strap hinges and wooden, site-built door handles.

Door 100: The opening is 6'-1½" by 8'-0 1/16". The original sliding door is fixed adjacent to the opening. The original door is plank and batten construction and has 4/4" by 5½" perimeter and diagonal bracing. Two temporary plywood, hinged, out-swinging doors with 1" by 6" nominal bracing have been installed in the historic east door opening by Park Service staff. There are two 3' by 7' custom-fabricated in-swinging screen doors installed on the interior part the doorframe. The casing is Type 1. There is no threshold at this opening.

Door 101: The frame opening is 3'-8" by 7'-4". There are two pintles on the western jamb of this opening, features from an earlier door. Door 101 is constructed of ¾" plywood with 1" by 4" nominal bracing and is mounted on the eastern jamb of the opening. There are three new steps constructed as part of the National Park Service stabilization work leading to this door. They are constructed of 8" risers and 11" treads to two 2" by 12" stringers. The head of the doorframe is Type 3, and the jamb is Type 2. There is no threshold at this opening.

Door 102: The frame opening is 3'-0 7/8" by 7'-3½". Door 102 is constructed of ¾" plywood with 1" by 4" nominal bracing. There is no physical evidence of an earlier door in this opening. The head of the doorframe is Type 2, and the jamb is Type 3. There is no threshold for this opening.

Door 103: This door and opening were under construction at the time of the site visit for this report. The rough opening is 3'-2 1/16" by 7'-0". There was no frame, threshold, or door associated with this opening at the time of the preparation of this report. However, the National Park Service Design Analysis for the stabilization and rehabilitation of the Seed House indicates that the door will be constructed of 1½" planed yellow pine planks with interior battens.

Door 104: At the time of the preparation of this report, there was no frame, threshold, or door for this opening. The rough opening is 2'-5-1/2"

Door 104: At the time of the preparation of this report, there was no frame, threshold, or door for this opening. The rough opening is 2'-5½" by 7'-10". The Design Analysis for the stabilization and rehabilitation of the Seed House indicates that the door will be constructed of 4/4" planed yellow pine planks with interior battens

Windows

The windows in the Seed House are on the north and south elevations of the east part of the structure. The windows did not originally have frames or sashes. Each has bottom-hinged, board-and-batten shutters. The shutters are constructed of four 4/4" horizontal wood planks of various widths with modern, galvanized strap hinges. At the time of the initial site visit for this report, all but one of the windows was fitted with an aluminum screen framed on plywood applied to the interior side of the window opening for pest/insect protection. In the winter of 2003, the National Park Service staff installed non-historic, interior, in-swinging casement windows with Plexiglas on five of the six windows in the east section of the Seed House. The National Park Service plans to install screens between the interior casement sashes and the historic shutters. These modifications are in response to the planned adaptive use of the structure for facility management.

In his description of the Seed House, Mr. Kenneth Prudhomme stated that the windows were for dust control and light, but, at times, were used as access to

Figure 28. Door 101.   Figure 29. Door 102.

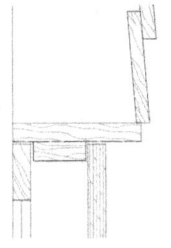 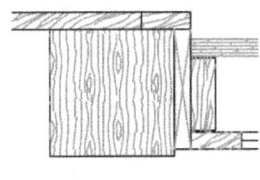

Figure 31. Head and Jamb 1

Figure 30. Head 2.

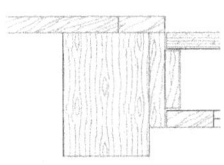 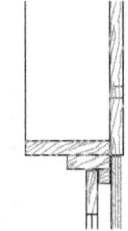

Figure 32. Jamb 2.

Figure 33. Head and Jamb 3.

shovel seed into wagons. In his memory, there were never frames or sashes in the windows. It is probable that the windows were used prior to and, in some cases, after, the Munger system was installed to load wagons transporting seed.

Window 100: The opening is 4'-8" by 2'-5". The dimension between the two adjacent wall framing posts defines the width of the window opening.

Window 101: The opening is 4'-5½" by 2'-10½". The dimension between the two adjacent wall framing posts defines the width of the window opening.

Window 102: The opening is 2'-2" by 2'-8". This window is notably smaller than the other windows in the east section of the Seed House and is in close proximity to the seed hopper. Its shutter is fixed shut due to the installation of a utility closet on the interior of the main structure. It appears that the

Figure 34. Window 100

Figure 35. Window 101

Figure 36. Window 102

Figure 37. Window 104

Figure 38. Window 103

Figure 39. Window 105

Figure 40. Seed Chute Shutters

function of this opening was originally somewhat different than the other windows in the east section of the Seed House due to its size and close proximity to the corner of the building.

Window 103: The opening is 3'-2" by 3'-9½". The dimension between the two adjacent wall framing posts defines the width of the window opening.

Window 104: The opening is 4'-4" by 2'-8". The dimension between the two adjacent wall framing posts defines the width of the window opening.

Window 105: This window is irregularly shaped and is temporarily covered in plywood.

Seed Chute Shutters: There are two top-hinged seed chute shutters of 4/4" by 8" vertical boards approximately 40" in length. The shutters have two battens on the inside. The historic boards have been reused in the reconstruction of these shutters by National Park Service staff, with in-kind materials replacing deteriorated or missing pieces.

Exterior Finish Materials and Characteristics
North Elevation: On the north elevation of the east section of the Seed House, the building is enclosed by horizontal plank siding installed on

the inside of the wall framing. The wall framing and plank siding are exposed on the exterior but are somewhat protected from the elements by the north shed roof. The siding on the west 14' portion of the north elevation is 1" by 8" clapboard siding with a 6½" exposure. The siding in this area appears to be mostly historic with new in-kind materials installed by Park Service staff to replace deteriorated or missing siding.

East Elevation: The east elevation is sided with 4/4" by 8" clapboard siding with a 6" exposure. The siding on this elevation is, for the most part, historic. Missing boards on this elevation were replaced by Park Service staff with the limited amount of sound siding available from the west elevation.

South Elevation: From Door 101 east (most of the east section of the building), there is no siding on the exterior. The wall framing is exposed on the exterior. From Door 101 to the joint between the east and west portions of the building, the siding is vertical 4/4" by 12" planks. From the joint between the east and west portions of the building to the west end of the south wall, the siding is 4/4" by 8" lap siding with a 6½" exposure.

West Elevation: The west elevation is 4/4" by 8"

clapboard siding with a 6½" exposure. This material
is new, but was installed by Park Service staff to
match the historic siding in dimension and species.

There is a shelf framed on the exterior of the seed
chute to divert seed into wagons. This shelf is
constructed of boards framed at an angle off the side
of the west elevation. The clapboard siding extends
up behind the shelf to enclose the wall.
Corner Boards: There are 4/4" by 5½" corner boards
located on each side of each of the four corners of the
Seed House. These were installed by National Park
Service staff as part of the rehabilitation work at the
Seed House. There was no physical evidence of
earlier corner boards prior to those installed by the
National Park Service.

Figure 41. Detail of exterior siding, east elevation.

Interior Finish Materials and Characteristics

Ceiling/ Underside of Roof
The eastern section of the interior of the Seed House
has exposed 2" by 6" circular sawn roof rafters and
wood roof sheathing. Historically, the metal roofing
panels were exposed to the interior through the gaps
between the roof sheathing. However, new building
felt installed above the sheathing by National Park
Service staff is visible from the interior of the
building.

The western portion of the interior, over the seed
chute, has double 2" by 4" circular sawn rafters that
replaced the single 2" by 4" rafters that were in place
at the time the National Park Service took possession
of the property. The double rafters were installed in
1999 at the recommendation of the Denver Service
Center Engineer. The height of the interior from the
floor to the top plate of the wall framing is
approximately 10' - 7". The distance from the top
plate to the ridge beam is 7'-5 5/8", resulting in an
overall interior height from the floor to the ridge of
18'. The roof sheathing of 4/4" by 12" boards spaced
with a 1" to 2" gap is historic. New building felt
installed above the sheathing by Park Service staff is
visible from the interior of the building.

Flooring
Plywood flooring measuring ¾" by 4' by 8' is
installed over the rehabilitated and supplemented
floor framing throughout the Seed House. The
present plywood flooring is intended to be a sub-
flooring in the completed rehabilitation work. The
planned finished floor is to be ¾" plywood sheets cut
into 12" wide strips to suggest the 12' plank flooring
originally used in the building. The Design Analysis
indicates the presence of 4/4" by 12" plank flooring
that no longer exists.

Figure 42. Detail of exterior siding, south elevation. Note the
differing materials on either side of the door.

Figure 43. Detail of roof rafters and sheathing, west end.

Figure 44. Floor detail.

Figure 45. Interior finishes, southwest corner.

Figure 46. Interior finishes, southeast corner.

Walls

North Wall: The east end of the north wall is horizontal, butt jointed 4/4" by 12" boards on the interior surface. The north interior wall has been substantially modified by the National Park Service from the historic wall assembly. The new wall assembly retains the historic exterior characteristics of the horizontal siding behind the exposed wall posts. On the inside of the exterior plank siding, a vapor barrier has been installed. On the inside of the vapor barrier is ¾" rigid insulation board, then a ½" layer of Homosote, a ¼" airspace, and the new, interior horizontal plank siding of dimensions matching the historic siding. The additional wall assembly is made possible by the installation of a 1½" vertical furring strip on the inside of each wall framing post.

South Wall: The east end of the south wall contains butt jointed 4/4" by 12" boards on the interior surface. The south wall in the area where the wall framing posts are exposed to the exterior is the same as that on the north wall.

The wall finish at the west end of the south wall, like the other exterior walls in the rehabilitated building, was modified from the historic assembly by the National Park Service. Historically, the interior of the wall was the exposed backside of the exterior clapboard siding. The modified wall assembly is designed to reduce moisture and wind infiltration in the building and to improve insulation for human occupancy in its facility management function. The modified wall section includes a vapor barrier on the inside of the clapboard siding, a layer of batt insulation supported by 2" by 4" studs and a ½" layer of Homosote exposed on the interior. This assembly is spaced to allow the timber wall framing to be exposed on the interior. building, was modified from the historic assembly by the National Park Service. Historically, the interior of the wall was the exposed backside of the exterior clapboard siding. The modified wall assembly is designed to reduce moisture and wind infiltration in the building and to improve insulation for human occupancy in its facility management function. The modified wall section includes a vapor barrier on the inside of the clapboard siding, a layer of batt insulation supported by 2" by 4" studs and a ½" layer of Homosote exposed on the interior. This assembly is spaced to allow the timber wall framing to be exposed on the interior.

East Wall: The east wall is similar to the historic and modified assembly of the west end of the south wall.

West Wall: The west wall is similar to the historic and modified assembly of the west end of the south wall.

Other Historic Features

Several historic seed-handling features of the Seed House have been retained. While they do not represent a complete assembly of the seed management process in the Seed House, they do provide interesting components from which one can gain some understanding of the operation of the Munger seed management equipment that was operated in the Seed House at Oakland Plantation.

Seed Intake Transition Fitting
at South Elevation

On the south side of the Seed House, to the west of center and under the shed roof, is a square to round galvanized transition fitting. This indicates the Seed House connecting point of the Munger seed transport pipe extending from the Gin Barn as shown in the c. 1905 photograph with the barn in the background. The location of the fitting is consistent with the characteristics in the historic photograph of the Gin Barn. It is known that the there was not a shed on the south side of the Seed House prior to 1905 from the c. 1905 photograph of the Seed House. There was a clear route for the seed pipe to travel from the Gin Barn to the Seed House and make the connection with the Seed House at the location of the existing fitting. The 1899 Munger catalog shows a fitting that matches the fitting on the side of the Seed House, confirming that it was a part of the Munger system. The transition fitting is galvanized metal and is in good condition due, in part, to having later been protected from the elements by the addition of the south shed roof.

Seed Chute

There are two seed chutes at the west end of the Seed House. The west expansion of the building was to accommodate a seed hopper. Six 6" by 6" circular sawn wooden columns on 2" by 8" framing that spans the columns and wall framing in the west wall of the Seed House support the seed chute. Two by six inch framing members spanning north to south above the 6" by 6" columns support the floor of the chute. The interior walls of the chute are vertical lap siding configured to encourage the movement of the seed from the chute through the chute doors and to the wagons. The chute floor sheathing is varied in size and age and ranged from aged 2" by 7" boards to some new 4/4" by 11" boards. The plank floor is butt jointed together with a 45 degree bevel.

Wooden Munger Seed Pipe and Iron Valve Lever

In the center of the west end of the building and extending from the hopper to the framing at the transition between the east and west portions of the building is an approximately 12" by 12" square wooden pipe. This pipe is one of only two remaining components of the Munger seed transport system

Figure 47. Interior finish of north wall.

Figure 48. Transition fitting located on south elevation.

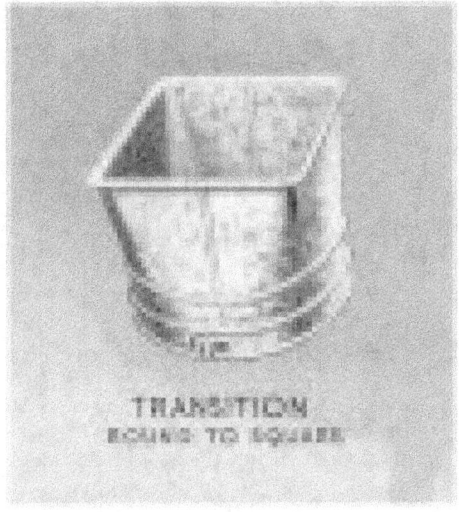

Figure 49. Transition from 1899 Munger Catalog, Continental Eagle, Inc., Prattville, AL.

Figure 50. Chute feeder pipe.

Figure 51. Two views of remaining equipment from Munger system stored at Oakland Plantation.

remaining in the Seed House. The other feature is the valve lever arm mounted below the south seed chute. A number of the Munger system seed handling components were in the Seed House at the time the National Park Service acquired the property. These

components are now stored in the shed behind the Main House. It is very likely that, with the number of existing historic Munger components already in the possession of the National Park Service, much of the Seed House Munger system could be reinstalled for interpretation.

Seed House Gutters

An examination of the c. 1905 photograph of the Seed House with the wagon in the foreground shows what appears to be a gutter system on the south side of the Seed House tied to an overhead trough or pipe extending in the direction of the Gin Barn and Cistern. The gutters appear to slope to a conductor-head like feature that is connected to the pipe. This photograph suggests the roof of the Seed House was used to supply rainwater to the Cistern. This observation must be qualified by the characteristics of the other c. 1905 photograph with the bale of cotton in the foreground and the Gin Barn in the background. This photograph shows the seed pipe but does not indicate any type of gutter feature that would be in the foreground of this photograph based on the observations of the Seed House photograph. The ultimate destination of the gutters on the Seed House in this photograph is unknown.

Modern Additions

The following features are part of the adaptive use program instituted by the National Park Service for the building and are all non-historic features. They are positioned on either side of the seed hopper, which is the most significant interpretative component in the Seed House.

Restroom: At the time of the site visit for this report, a restroom was being framed in the northwest corner of the Seed House. Only the rough framing was in place. The framing extends to 9' in height, not the full height of the building. The location of the restroom is on the side of the building closest to where the utilities enter the site. This feature does not contribute to the historic character of the building and, indeed, impedes understanding of the historic remnants of the seed-handling system on the west end of the building.

Storage Room: To the east of the restroom and adjacent to it, 2" by 4" framing to 9' in height for a small storage was also in place at the time of the initial site visit for this report. This room is also part of the adaptive use program instituted by the National Park Service for this building. This feature does not contribute to the historic character of the building.

Storage Lockers: A series of 8'-tall storage lockers are positioned in the southwest corner of the Seed House. It appears that they are not attached in any significant or damaging way to the building, thereby being reversible should their removal be desired in the future. Due to the stabilization and rehabilitation completed to date, the Seed House is in excellent condition. While the adaptive use modifications made for the facility management operations have introduced non-historic features, overall, the volume of the building, its exterior finishes, and the remaining components of the seed handling apparatus are intact, allowing interpretation of the building while achieving functional operational use of the building.

UTILITY YARD

There were no utilities in the building at the time of the site visit. An extension cord from a ground-mounted power pedestal on the west side of the building was powering the lights and a fan inside the building. However, it appeared that the building was being readied for power, water, and sewer service. The collection of site utility features to the west of the building appear to be in place to support the adaptive use planned for the structure by the National Park Service. Overall, these features are low to the ground and present as low a profile as can be expected.

PAINT ANALYSIS

The finishes on the Seed House are unpainted. None of the existing features on the Gin Complex site are painted. Therefore, a paint analysis was not done for the Seed House or the remaining Gin Complex site features.

ELECTRICAL EVALUATION

There was no existing electrical service in the Seed House at the time the National Park Service acquired the property. All utilities currently servicing the Seed House have been installed by the National Park Service. Underground electrical service with pad-mounted transformer and meter was installed. The electrical service for the Seed House currently consists of the following (as of the writing of this report):

Interior:
- An extension cord runs from the new meter outlet, utilizing a 30A circuit breaker, to the structure.
- Surface/pendant mounted incandescent light fixtures are mounted on the bottom of the roof structure beams and connected together with extension cords.

Exterior:
- The main disconnect switch, with no rated

Figure 53. Utility Yard.

Figure 52. Framing for restroom and storage room in Seed House.

voltage and current shown on the label.
- A pump disconnect switch for the new wastewater pump, with no rated voltage and current shown on the label.
- A waste water pump and control panel.
- ¾" PVC Sch. 40 underground service entrance conduit to main disconnect switch.
- Conduits, elbow connections, and fittings between the disconnect switches and wastewater pump inadequately supported.

The existing electrical service is inadequate for future use of the Seed House as a workshop or maintenance facility and does not comply with current National Electrical Code requirements and standards. It is understood that this electrical system is intended by the Park Service to be temporary and will be upgraded in the future.

Bibliography

Breedlove, Carolyn. "Bermuda/Oakland Plantation, 1830-1880." Unpublished masters thesis. Northwestern State University of Louisiana, 1999.

Britton, Karen Gerhardt. *Bale o' Cotton, The Mechanical Art of Cotton Ginning.* College Station: Texas A&M University Press, 1992.

Census Records of the United States, Seventh through Tenth, and Twelfth through Fifteenth, 1850, 1860, 1870, 1880, 1900, 1910, 1920, and 1930, Population Schedules, Natchitoches Parish, Louisiana. Reviewed online at Ancestry.com. 2001 and 2002.

Deblieux, Robert B. *"Cane River Country, 'La Cote Joyeuse' and Kisatchie National Forest. An Auto Guide to the Historically and Architecturally Important Plantations of Creole Origins and a Guide to the vistas, Hiking Trails and Flora of the Forest of Natchitoches Parish.* Natchitoches: The Natchitoches Times, 1993.

DeBlieux, Robert B. *"Natchitoches – A Guide to the Historically and Architecturally Important Buildings in the Historic District.* Natchitoches: The Natchitoches Times, 1989.

Firth, Ian, Professor, School of Environmental Design, University of Georgia at Athens. Oral interview with Deborah Harvey, September 9, 2002.

Firth, Ian. "Cultural Landscape Report – Oakland Plantation." Draft manuscript undertaken for the National Park Service, unpublished.

Ford, Eric Z. *Design Analysis – Rehabilitation of the Seed House for Adaptive Reuse, Oakland Plantation.* Natchez: National Park Service, U.S. Department of the Interior, 2001.

Fortier, Alcee, ed. "Jacques Alphonse Prud'homme," *Louisiana, Comprising Sketches of Counties, Towns, Events, Institutions, and Persons Arranged in Cyclopedic Form,* Atlanta: Southern Historical Association, 1909.

Fricker, Jonathan. *National Register of Historic Places – Oakland Plantation Addendum.*

National Register of Historic Places, 1989.

Malone, Ann Patton, Ph.D. Series of oral history interviews conducted between 1996-1997 with members of the extended Prud'homme family and their workers. Individual citation states name of interviewee.

Malone, Ann Patton, Ph.D. "Oakland Plantation, Its People's Testimony." Draft of oral history project. Unpublished. 1998.

National Park Service. *Cane River Creole National Historical Park Draft General Management Plan/Environmental Impact Statement,* Denver: U.S. Department of the Interior, 2001.

Pace, Seneca. "Daily Record of Passing Events on Prud'homme Plantation, 1860," Prud'homme Family Papers, Series 3.1.5, Plantation Journals and Records, 1788-1997, Southern Historical Collection, Wilson Library, University of North Carolina, Chapel Hill, North Carolina.

Prud'homme, Alphonse. Farm journals for 1866, Prud'homme Family Papers, Series 3.1.5, Plantation Journals and Records, 1788-1997, Southern Historical Collection, Wilson Library, University of North Carolina, Chapel Hill, North Carolina.

Prudhomme, Mrs. James Alphonse (Lucile K.), and Mr. and Mrs. R. L. Williamson. *National Register of Historic Places Inventory – Nomination Form.* National Register of Historic Places, 1978.

Prudhomme, Kenneth. Oral interview with Mr. Jack Pyburn, AIA, of The Office of Jack Pyburn, Architect, Inc., 2003.

Prudhomme, Mrs. Lucile K., comp. "Prud'homme-Keator Family Bible." Genealogical information entered by Lucile Keator Prud'homme on the Prud'homme and Lambre families.

Prudhomme, Mrs. Lucile K., comp. "The Prud'homme Family" Genealogical information on the descendants of Jean Pierre Phillippe Prud'homme and his wife, Catherine Mesilier. Unpublished.

Drawings

Drawings

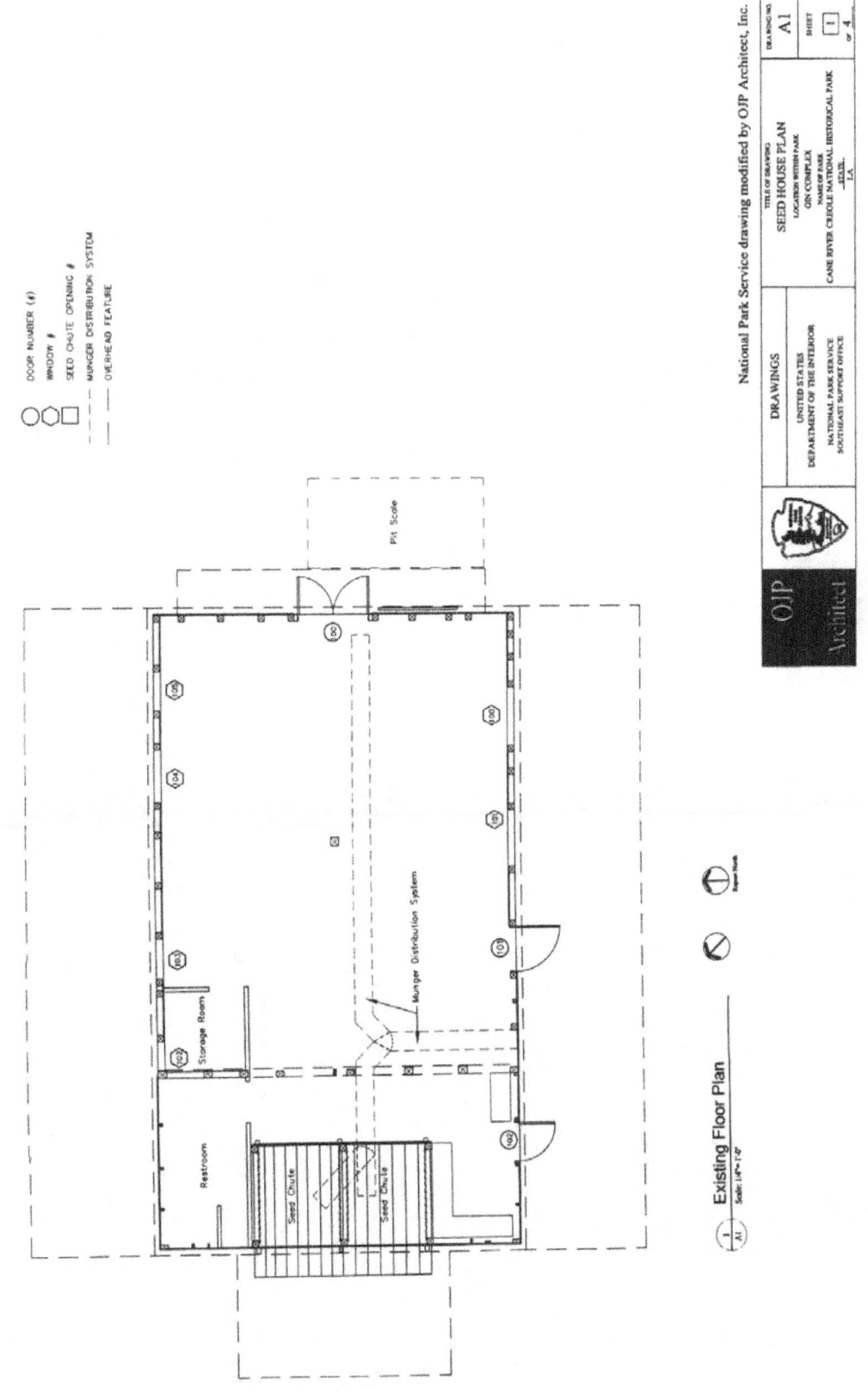

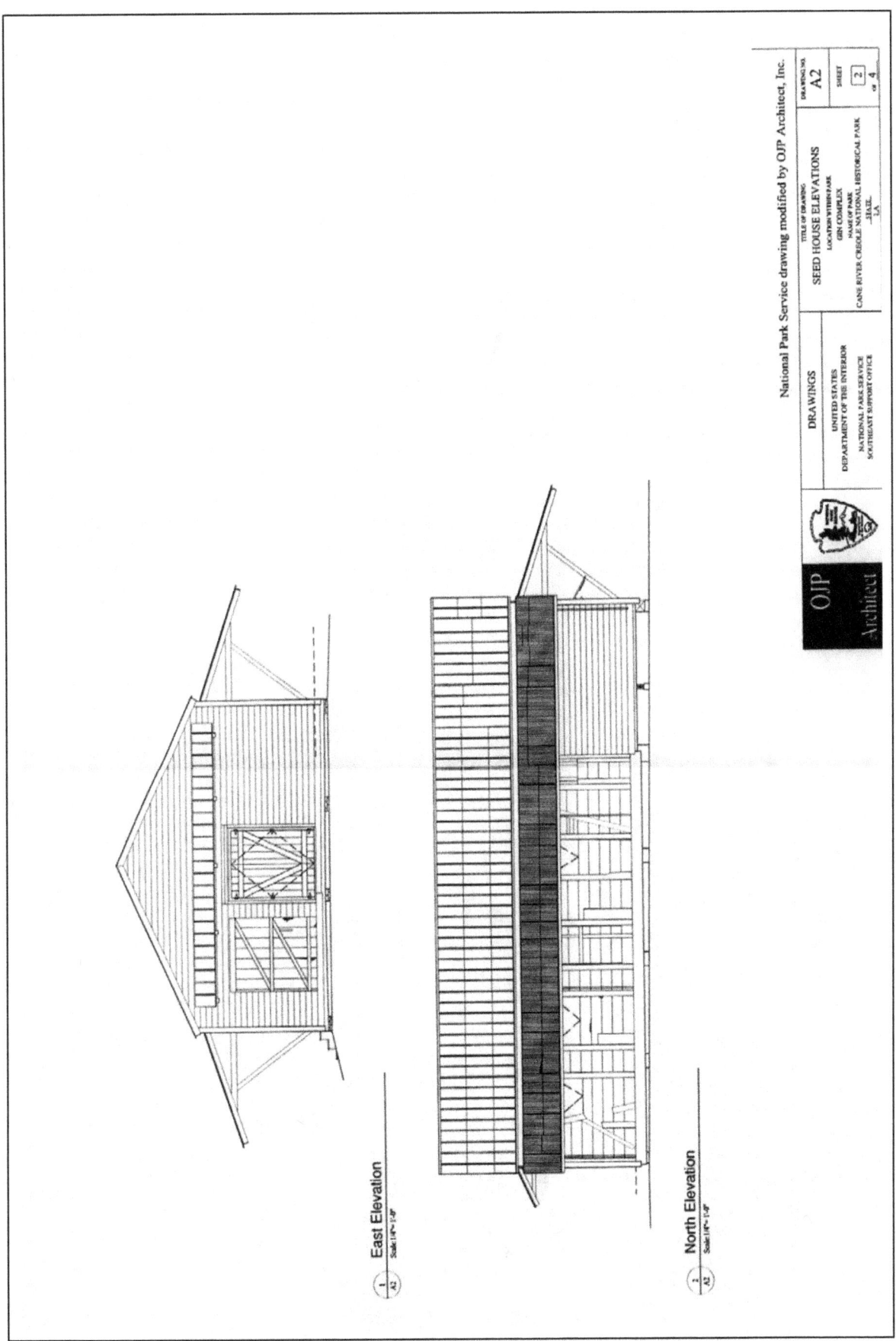

East Elevation

North Elevation

National Park Service drawing modified by OJP Architect, Inc.

DRAWINGS

SEED HOUSE ELEVATIONS

CANE RIVER CREOLE NATIONAL HISTORICAL PARK

A2

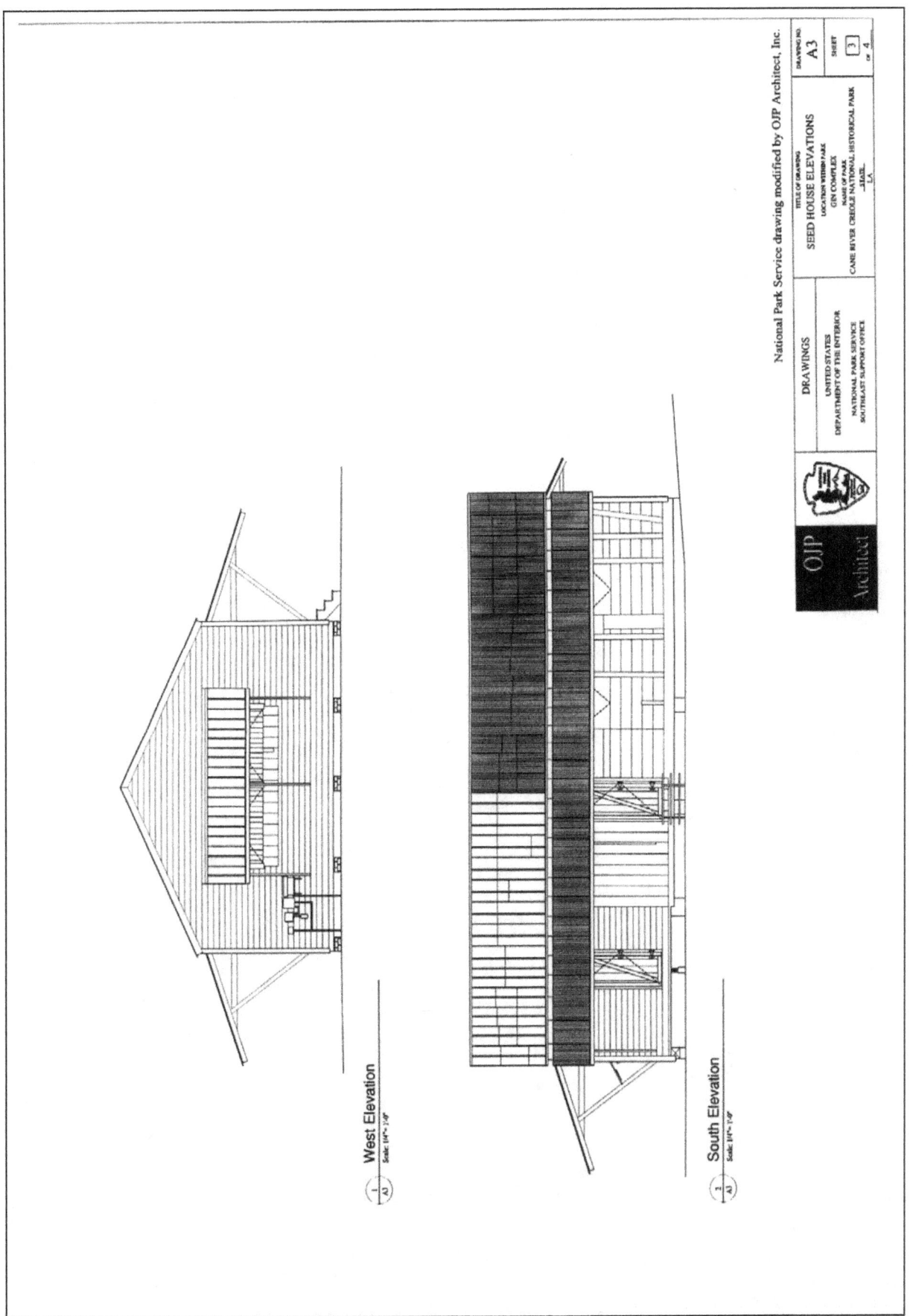

Drawings

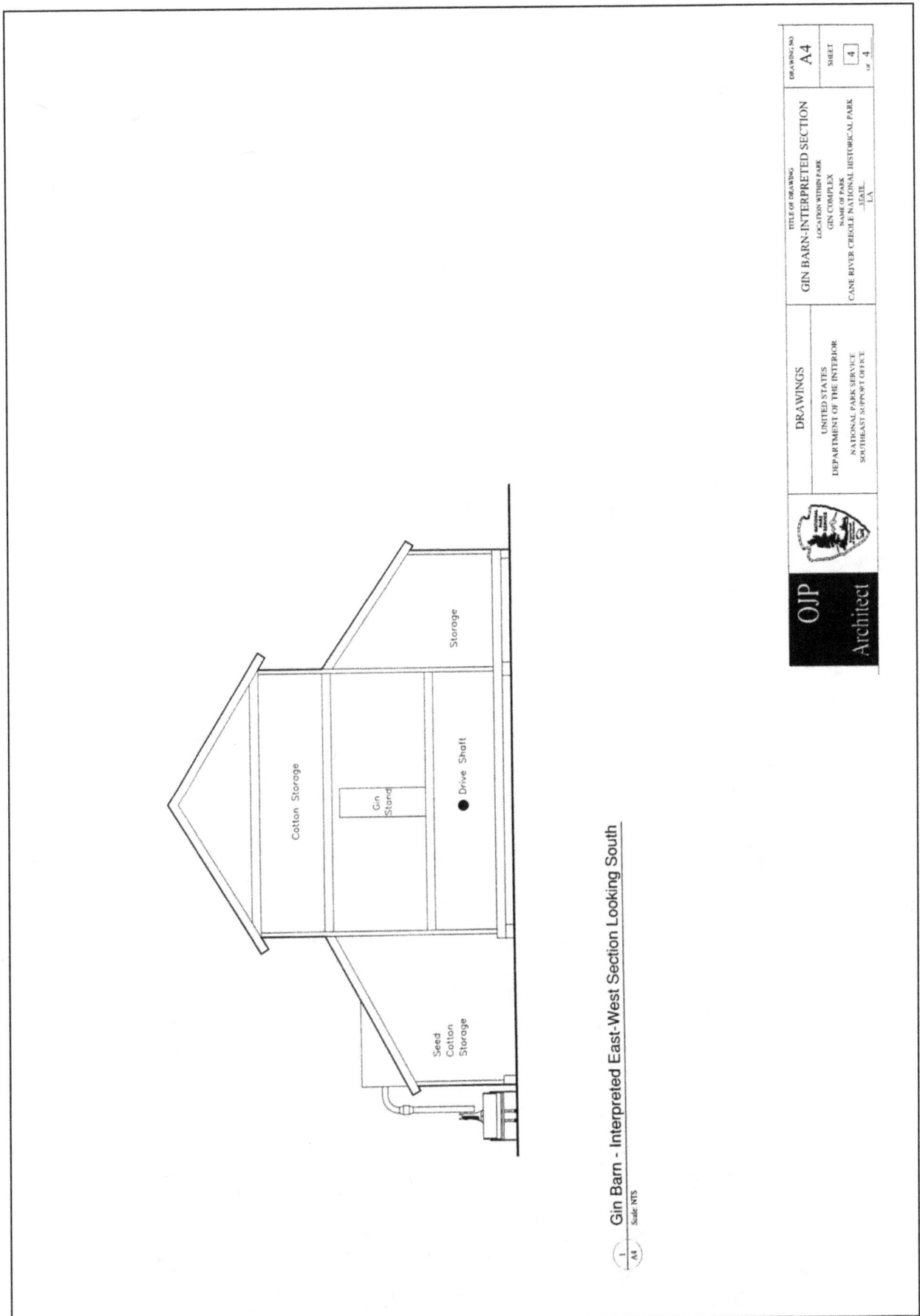

Gin Barn - Interpreted East-West Section Looking South

Drawings

PART II: TREATMENT AND USE

Oakland Gin HSR

Treatment and Use

The Seed House is the primary structure remaining from the last of three gin complexes on Oakland Plantation. Other surviving features include the Cistern, gin-related machinery foundations, and portions of the seed handling equipment. During the period of economic viability of cotton production, the gin was the mechanical heart of the plantation. With the loss of the Gin Barn and the ginning machinery, the Seed House takes on added significance as the visual feature with which ginning can be interpreted.

The General Management Plan (GMP) for the park has assigned the adaptive use of indoor maintenance to the Seed House in Phase One of the plan implementation. Under Phase Two of the GMP, the Seed House is to be used for educational functions. The timing for the introduction of educational functions and the specific scope of the educational functions are not defined in the GMP. However, the approach to treatment of the Seed House should be determined by its proposed ultimate use.

Before this Historic Structure Report was undertaken, the Seed House had received significant modifications to accommodate the maintenance functions that it was assigned. These treatments are outlined in detail in the September 2001 Design Analysis written by the National Park Service. The structure had been stabilized with new piers, the floor leveled with sistered supplementary framing to the original floor beams, and the original wall framing was stabilized and insulated. Two non-historic rooms are being added to the interior: a storage room and a restroom that meets the Americans with Disabilities Act (ADA) standards (at this time, the building is not ADA accessible). Due to extensive restoration and rehabilitation treatments that have already been undertaken, it is difficult for the average visitor to visually discern which remaining components of the building are original.

It is presumed that the current appearance of the exterior of the Seed House is similar to the 1960 appearance. This is the designated end of the Period of Significance. It appears that the original framing, seed hopper, and wood pipe on the west end of the structure are the most significantly intact components of the building. Given the extent of modifications made for the proposed adaptive use of the Seed House, focus on the remaining historically significant components will be of limited value.

Requirements for Use

The requirements for converting the Seed House from a support building for cotton production to a National Park Service management and maintenance facility have resulted in significant building modifications. The treatment of the Seed House appears to have been accomplished with consideration of its historic character but with limited information regarding its relationship to the larger Gin Complex. With limited information, particularly archeological, on the Gin Complex, the rehabilitation and adaptive use decisions could not take into account the effect of the rehabilitation actions on understanding and interpreting the larger complex.

Field observations suggest that the management and maintenance functions to be housed by the Seed House will include wood fabrication, finish tool storage, limited material storage, and staff restrooms and lockers. The shed roofs on the sides of the main structure are providing weather protection for equipment and some supplies. The management and maintenance function will require adequate floor loading capacity for the weight of equipment and material to be accommodated in the building. The single unisex restroom will likely suffice for the occupancy of the building in its proposed Phase One use. ADA compliant accessibility is currently not provided to the building, but will be required.

Requirements for an educational use of the Seed House are considerably different from the maintenance use. For educational purposes, the retention of historically significant features for interpretation is more important. Restroom facility requirements are more demanding. However, there is no plan to add a second restroom to this building when it is converted to an educational use. Presumably, lighting and interpretative support will then be desired. Accessibility from parking to the main Seed House room will be more critical.

Requirements for Treatment

Section 106 of the National Historic Preservation Act (NHPA) mandates that federal agencies, including the National Park Service, take into account the effects of their actions on properties listed in or eligible for listing in the National Register of Historic Places (NRHP) and give the Advisory Council on Historic Preservation a reasonable opportunity to comment on proposed treatments. NHPA regulations (36 CFR 800.10) mandate special requirements for the protection of National Historic Landmarks. Section 110(f) of the Act requires that the Agency Official, to the maximum extent possible, undertake such planning and actions as may be necessary to minimize harm to any National Historic Landmark that may be directly and adversely affected by any undertaking. The National Park Service's "Cultural Resource Management Guideline" (DO 28) requires planning for the protection of cultural resources whether or not they relate to the specific authorizing legislation or interpretive programs of the parks in which they lie. The Seed House should be understood in its own cultural context and managed in light of its own value, relative to the Gin Complex of which it was originally a part, as well as to Oakland Plantation as a whole, so that it may be preserved and rehabilitated, unimpaired, for the enjoyment of present and future generations. To help guide compliance with these statutes and regulations, the Secretary of the Interior has issued *Standards for the Treatment of Historic Properties.* The National Park Service's *Preservation Briefs* also provide detailed guidelines for appropriate treatment of a variety of materials, features, and conditions found in historic buildings.

The primary component of the National Park Service mission for the Seed House is to implement an adaptive use for the building that respects its historic integrity. Understanding the history of the buildings and structures that comprised the ginning function of Oakland Plantation is key to the proper treatment and use of the Seed House. It was in recognition of both the historic integrity and significance of Oakland Plantation that the National Park Service wrote the General Management Plan for its care. The General Management Plan discusses several use alternatives for the Seed House. In all but one of the alternatives, the proposed use of the Seed House is to house facility management operations during the first phase of park operations. Upon completion of Phase One, the Seed House will be adapted for use as an educational facility during the second phase of park operations.

When the National Park Service acquired the Seed House, it was in a deteriorated state due to age, animal and insect infestation, invasive vegetation, and general neglect. In 1999, the building underwent stabilization and preservation treatments by the Historic Preservation Training Center (HPTC) and Cane River Creole National Historic Park (CARI). Most of these treatments are discussed in the "Chronology of Development and Use" and the "Physical Description" sections of this report. In September 2001, the National Park Service wrote a Design Analysis on the seed house entitled

Rehabilitation of the Seed House for Adaptive Reuse – Oakland Plantation. The purpose of this Design Analysis and Description was to present the existing condition of the building and the measures needed to rehabilitate it for the proposed Phase One adaptive use. This report did not address the Phase Two proposed use for education and the implications of Phase One improvements on the Phase Two use.

The report notes that many of the identified treatments and modifications were completed as part of the 1999 efforts of HPTC and CARI. Those completed include the rehabilitation of existing building features, as well as the replacement of deteriorated features with in-kind materials. The features that were modified for the adaptive use comprised most of the building and include the foundation piers, floor, wall and roof framing, gabled and shed roofing materials, and portions of the exterior wall finishes. The report also recommended other treatments including installing insulation and vapor barriers in the walls and roof, new sub-flooring and finished flooring, new interior plank walls where needed, new windows, and new doors. Some of these treatments were underway at the time of the initial site visit for the preparation of this Historic Structure Report.

While the Federal Government is not bound by state and local building codes, the National Park Service typically respects their existence. In doing so, they consider the relationship of all proposed modifications to state and local codes, where applicable. The identified local codes in Natchitoches Parish include:

- Building Code: 2000 International Building Code (IBC)
- Electrical Code: National Electrical Code (NEC)
- Mechanical Code: International Plumbing Code (IPC), International Mechanical Code (IMC)
- Fire Protection Code: National Fire Protection Code (NFPC)

It is not clear if the Seed House modifications made to date have undergone a review for state and local code compliance.

Structural analysis of augmented floor framing of the Seed House's indicates that, according to modern building codes, the current framing is not adequate to support maintenance and storage such as that observed in the structure during the site investigation visits in 2002 and 2003. Conversations with Park personnel indicate that the intended use of the building is as an office and assembly area for maintenance personnel at the Park. In addition, the Phase II proposed use as an educational facility may require greater load capacity than currently exists at the Seed House, depending on the type of educational facility. It is necessary to further strengthen the floor framing of the Seed House to accommodate its current use as a maintenance and light carpentry facility. It may be necessary to strengthen the floor framing if the Park desires to meet current building codes for future uses of the building, as well. Alternatives to strengthening of the floor framing system are discussed in the "Ultimate Treatment" section of this report.

For the management and maintenance function, the Seed House requires restroom facilities accessible per the requirements of the Americans with Disabilities Act (ADA), ADA compliant access to the building, and compliant signage. Based on the maintenance staff occupancy, it appears that the single accessible restroom being installed in the Seed House will be adequate to accommodate the management and maintenance functions. It is expected to be the used to support future educational functions as well.

Given the maintenance and management functions in the Seed House, the elevation of the above grade flooring, and the functional requirements of the proposed uses, an ADA compliant ramp is an appropriate approach to satisfying ADA accessibility requirements. Plans incorporated in the Design Analysis report prepared by the National Park Service locate a ramp along the east end of the south façade under the shed providing access to the interior through Door 101. Only the south and east elevations have existing door openings. The west elevation is constrained by the presence of the seed hopper feature that spans the west wall. The north wall is, in fact, the one most convenient to the parking that has been installed to the north of the building, but it appears to have not had doors in its earlier, historically significant configuration. The east elevation is fitted with an historic sliding door that is a character-defining feature and is currently in a fixed position beside the opening. A pair of temporary plywood doors secures the opening in this wall. This opening is approximately 8' wide and will be necessary for moving oversized equipment and materials into and out of the building during the proposed Phase One use. However, locating a ramp at this opening would partially obscure the door and impact the historic character of the building. The south elevation has two door openings, both of which meet ADA width requirements. Considering the size and orientation of the building with respect to its historic function and interpretive potential, locating a ramp on the south elevation would have the least impact on the overall presentation of the rehabilitated building for interpretation.

According to the September 2001 National Park Service Design Analysis report, all adaptive use work

involving mechanical, electrical, telephone, and lighting protection will be, "mounted only to extant joints, timbers, and planks." It was observed during the initial Historic Structure Report site visit that furring strips and building felt had been applied to some interior walls. The Design Analysis report recommended the modification of the building's wall assembly to assist in the interior comfort of the occupied building prior to the installation of new wall finishes in the interior.

There was no information on the presence of hazardous materials in the building. Because the building was not painted, lead-containing paint does not appear to be an issue. As there were no mechanical or electrical systems originally in the building, it is unlikely that there are any PCBs or asbestos associated with the building. The primary potential sources for contaminants in a building such as the Seed House are materials, chemicals, and components associated with the late years of ginning that might have permeated the soil. However, there is no evidence in the records that such conditions existed.

Fire protection is an issue in both the Phase One and proposed Phase Two uses. The use of power tools, space heaters, and other related equipment that can generate a spark or heat are items that should be handled with fire prevention in mind. Given the relatively small size of the building and travel distance to the exterior, a pressurized fire protection system appears unwarranted. However, the judicious placement of the proper type of portable extinguishers and smoke alarms are appropriate fire protection measures. The existence of three exits, one of them oversized, allow for no restrictions on occupancy based on issues of life safety. Issues of occupancy are based on the amount of available floor space and the strength of the floor framing system.

The Seed House will not have a central heating system. It will be an unconditioned space with the exception of space heaters and fans. The exterior walls of the building have been insulated to improve the comfort of the building. With this improvement, there will be some minor energy savings over the original, open, un-insulated condition of the Seed House.

Alternatives for Treatment

The Seed House has already been significantly modified to accommodate management and maintenance functions at the site. Therefore, there is not an opportunity to address the alternatives to that use and the implications for alternative uses on the building's historic fabric. However, the proposed Phase Two use for educational purposes can be addressed here. There seem to be two alternatives to the educational use: 1) keeping the Seed House in management/maintenance use for the long term, and 2) finding an alternative use for the Seed House other than maintenance and management. Keeping the Seed House in maintenance and management use would not precipitate any difficulties to the remaining historic fabric of the building if the floor loads were maintained within the capacity of the historic floor framing. However, this may be a limitation deemed undesirable for the long term as the demands for maintenance increase with visitation to the park. The need to have significant floor loads on the building will likely increase with the visitation and maintenance activities.

Though the historic fabric of the Seed House has been significantly altered, the ultimate use of the Seed House for educational functions appears to have merit. First, there has been sufficient alteration to the Seed House that public use will not threaten the original building fabric. While effort has been given to replacing the interior and exterior building shell with materials matching the original, it appears that only the historic heavy timber framing is significantly intact. Short of overloading the floor framing capacity, the timber framing can withstand supervised heavy public use. The ADA ramp installed for the maintenance function would be functional for public educational programs.

A valid case for the using the Seed House for educational purposes is that it is one of the last of two remaining structures of the Oakland Gin Complex. The building is important for interpreting the significance of the Gin Complex to the years of cotton production on the plantation. Interpreting cotton production is important for understanding the significance of the arrangement, and even the existence, of the entire plantation. In addition to the opportunity to interpret ginning at Oakland, there is also an opportunity to communicate the relationship of the ginning operation at Oakland Plantation with the ginning operation at Magnolia Plantation. Together, the two plantations present a more complete interpretation of the heart of the plantation, the cotton gin operation. Without the Seed House, interpretation is limited to media presentations or docent explanations out on the site.

The newly-installed maintenance restroom, storage room, and removable lockers obscure some of the remaining seed handling features in the seed house. With these new additions, the hopper and wood supply pipe are in an unfortunate location for seed handing interpretation if the building were used for education. Therefore, some reversal of the current improvements may be merited, such as removing the modern restrooms from the Seed House and

providing alternative facilities in an appropriate location elsewhere. Any required storage could be freestanding in the room and integrated with the exhibits and media projection equipment. Interpretative opportunities for this structure: Early construction methods are easily discerned in the hewn, heavy timber framing that is visible from both the interior and the exterior.
Operation of a Seed House as it relates to the overall Gin Complex could be demonstrated, especially if the Munger system components currently in the possession of the National Park Service were re-installed in the Seed House. With the Magnolia Gin Barn, the Park would thus be able to interpret the entire cotton processing system.

Reconstruction of the Gin Barn and steam and diesel engine houses according to historic records could be undertaken. This would be costly and would necessitate further archaeological research used in conjunction with aerial photographs to determine the historic placement of the buildings.

Ultimate Treatment and Use

The ultimate use of the Seed House for educational functions appears to be a good choice. Given the work on the building to adapt it for maintenance functions, there are limited rehabilitation and restoration actions appropriate or necessary to convert the Seed House from a maintenance use to an educational use. They include:

Restoration: Some restoration of the seed hopper and wood supply pipe should be considered. There appear to be sufficient intact components to facilitate the interpretation of seed transport to the planting wagons on the west side of the building. The Munger seed handling system could be re-installed in the Seed House using the components currently in the possession of the National Park Service and reconstructing missing components as necessary. The relationship of the seed handling system to the larger ginning process should be clearly interpreted using media such as exhibits and graphics.

Preservation: The east sliding door and hardware, the seed hopper and wood supply pipe, and the building's remaining historic wooden components, including the heavy timber frame, should be preserved.

Rehabilitation: The rehabilitation of the Seed House is substantially complete. The General Management Plan defines the Phase I use of the Seed House as a Park maintenance facility. Discussions with Park personnel indicate that, although the building currently houses carpentry equipment such as a table saw as well as some materials storage, the main use of the building under the facilities management designation would be as an office and assembly area for maintenance personnel. However, the reconstruction of the floor framing of the building, which was accomplished by replacing the deteriorated portions of the floor framing and adding some supplemental strengthening, does not meet current building codes for loads in offices. The Park Service plans to convert the space for use as an educational facility when it becomes inadequate as a maintenance facility. What kind of educational facility this would be is unclear. Reinstalling the Munger system in the Seed House for purposes of allowing tour groups to view it could result in a use defined by the International Building Code as an assembly area. The floor framing as it currently exists does not meet current building code requirements for assembly areas, 100 psf. However, the load requirement for a classroom, which would include students, chairs, and desks, is 40 psf, the load the floor framing system can currently withstand based on the computer-modeled structural analysis of the system.

Three methods could be used to mitigate the problem of the floor framing not adhering to code with regard to the current and proposed uses of the Seed House. One is to strengthen the existing floor framing. This strengthening would not involve removal of any historic materials, but would involve installation of supplemental material. This supplemental support would be joists installed beneath and perpendicular to existing joists and attached to existing piers to reduce the span between joists and provide vertical support. It should be noted that much of the existing floor framing was installed between 1999 and 2002 by the National Park Service during rehabilitation efforts at the Seed House. Consequently, there is not a significant amount of remaining historic material in the floor framing system. Strengthening the floor framing would not result in any degradation of the existing visual presentation because all strengthening would be installed beneath the existing floor and would, therefore, not be visible to the casual observer. There would be some expense associated with this approach. Drawings showing modifications to the floor framing that would provide the strength required by code have been prepared by Hartrampf, Inc. for the use of the National Park Service, should the Park choose this method. However, these drawings are not included with this report because this is not the preferred method of dealing with the structural needs of the Seed House to accommodate the proposed uses as outlined in the General Management Plan for the Park. If the National Park Service desires to strengthen the floor framing beneath the floor, the Park Service should contact Hartrampf, Inc. to obtain these drawings.

The second method is to restrict the load on the floor framing. As it currently exists, the floor can withstand a load of 40 psf (pounds per square foot) based on the computer-modeled structural analysis of the framing. The code requirement for an office space is a load of 60 psf. To avoid strengthening the floor framing to meet current building codes, the Park must restrict the weight of stored materials and equipment to 40 psf. To do this, the Park will need to monitor the weight of items stored in the building as well as the weight and locations of office equipment such as desks, copiers, and file cabinets. Heavier items, such as copiers, desks, or light maintenance equipment such as the table saw, should be positioned over a pier. Personnel should be instructed in the reason for the locations of the heavier office equipment and not be allowed to move them at random. This option would require frequent monitoring of the loads to which the floor framing system is subjected.

The third method is to stiffen the floor with the addition of another layer of plywood sheathing. Discussions with on-site National Park Service staff at Oakland Plantation indicate that there are plans to add another layer of plywood sheathing to the floor. If this layer is added, the Seed House floor and its supporting members will be adequate for a live load of 60 psf, but not for an assembly load of 100 psf. The additional flooring must have a minimum thickness of ¾ inch and be securely fastened to the floor joists using minimum 10d common nails spaced no more than 16" on center. For the Seed House to function as office space per the Park's General Management Plan without strengthening the floor framing system from below, this additional plywood sheathing must be added to the floor. This method would be much less expensive than the first method mentioned and would allow the Park to use the Seed House as proposed under the General Management Plan with fewer limitations than the second method. With the additional flooring, the Seed House can support a live load of 60 psf, which meets current codes for office, fixed-seat assembly, and classroom occupancy. This method is, therefore, preferred to the first two methods because it is the simplest method, is less expensive than the first alternative, and is already part of the rehabilitation plan for the Seed House.

When the Park converts the Seed House to an educational facility, the building code requirements for public assembly space (100 psf) or for classroom space (40 psf) will apply. Which load applies depends on the configuration of the educational function of the building. However, in both cases, restricting the number of people in the building can eliminate the need to strengthen the floor framing. To determine the maximum number of people that should be allowed inside the building simultaneously, the allowable capacity as determined by the analysis (40 psf) was multiplied by the available floor area of the building and divided by 400, which is the International Building Code (IBC) standard 300-lb person multiplied by the standard IBC impact factor of 1.3. To avoid additional strengthening of the floor framing, the number of people in the building should be limited to one hundred people, assuming maintenance equipment and storage has been removed. Park Service personnel would need to ensure that storage of educational equipment and supplies does not exceed 40 psf. If the Park Service chooses to add the extra layer of plywood sheathing rather than strengthen the floor framing system from below, the number of people allowed in the building at one time should not exceed one hundred and fifty.

If the Park does not add and attach the extra layer of plywood to the floor, a fourth means of reconciling the strength of the existing floor framing with the use of the building would be to change the proposed use to one that does not exceed the limits of the current floor framing. For instance, the building code requirements for a classroom, with students, chairs, and desks, is 40 psf, the load that the current floor framing system can accommodate without modification. This is because the addition of chairs and desks in a uniform configuration, such as in rows, restricts the number of units that can be accommodated in the structure and spreads the load more uniformly across the framing system. However, this approach would require that the Park locate the current maintenance facility elsewhere, as the required load capacity for offices (60 psf) exceeds the existing load capacity of the floor framing system (40 psf).

The work required to strengthen the floor framing system of the Seed House to meet code requirements would add non-historic materials. Strengthening of the structure from below would be more costly than other means of meeting the floor load demands. Strengthening the floor framing system by adding an extra layer of ¾" plywood flooring would be the simplest method of addressing current building code requirements, though not the least expensive. Abandoning the use of the building as a maintenance facility may not meet the needs of the Park. It is entirely feasible to manage the load on the existing floor framing to avoid overstressing it without seriously restricting the capability of the structure to meet its current planned use or its future planned use. Therefore, the recommendation is to not modify the existing floor system from below. The preferred approach is to apply the extra layer of plywood to the existing floor and restrict the amount of load allowed on the floor system as discussed, either by restricting the number of people and the amount of equipment and storage allowed in the building or by converting the building to another use, such as a classroom.

Upgrading of electrical equipment to meet code requirements: The electrical connections in existence during the initial site visit for this report are considered temporary. The following are the recommendations of the Hartrampf, Inc. electrical engineer who inspected the site. These recommendations are based on the understanding of the purpose and function of the future facility usage as a maintenance facility. The installations must be made in compliance with the latest National Electrical Code standards and all local regulations. Electrical service should be sized according to the differing electrical load requirements for the proposed equipment. To minimize intrusion into the remaining historic fabric and to make the improvements reversible if desired later, electrical components should be surface-mounted.

- Install service entrance conductors and conduits from the secondary side of the utility transformer to service entrance equipment located in a designated area with appropriate ventilation.
- Surface-mount electrical panels with appropriate number and sizes of circuit breakers for the various loads required for equipment.
- Surface-mount light fixtures with energy-saving features; surface-mount conduits to serve these fixtures.
- Surface-mount receptacles throughout the building; surface-mount conduits and junction boxes to serve these fixtures.
- Surface-mount telephone backboard; connect with underground conduit from telephone company to the building.
- Surface-mount telephone and data outlets throughout the building; surface-mount conduits to serve these fixtures.
- Surface-mount exterior receptacles (GFCI) with weatherproof covers; surface-mount conduits to serve these fixtures.
- Surface-mount exterior light fixtures around building; surface mount conduits to serve these fixtures.
- Install an underground grounding ring or ground rods around building to bond all metal and electrical components to one grounding system.
- Install lightning protection above the roof and bond to the grounding system.
- Surface-mount any heating or cooling devices, such as wall heaters or ceiling fans; surface-mount conduits to serve these features.

Adaptive Measures: Remove the recently-built restroom and storage room to better open the Seed House for interpretation and education.

Other Recommended Actions:
Additional archaeological research in the Gin Complex area. Archeological research in the area of the Gin Complex is recommended to augment the current understanding of the arrangement of the missing features and their relationship to the existing ones.

Additional research into Oakland Plantation records regarding the Gin Complex. A better understanding of the relationship of the Gin and its related buildings to the functioning of the plantation after the Civil War could be obtained by a more thorough examination of documents both in the possession of the National Park Service and of other institutions than could be made during the course of the investigation for this report. Many of the early documents are in French and would require careful interpretation. Other locations where pertinent documents may exist include the hardware store in downtown Natchitoches, which has been in continuous operation since the Civil War and claims to have the sales receipts to prove it, and records of the insurance companies that insured the equipment for the plantation.

Catalog, store, and preserve all components identified as part of the Oakland Plantation Gin Complex that are not used or replaced in their original locations for interpretation. This includes the parts of the Munger system currently located on site, and any features that can be retrieved, such as the diesel engine currently being used as a roadside ornament at the Cane River Gin on Highway 494 in Natchitoches.

The Gin Complex did not operate without workers. Some workers at the Oakland Plantation ginning operation have been peripherally documented. Further genealogical research into these families, particularly the Helaires and the Nargots, should be undertaken to further aid in the interpretation of the plantation as a whole.

While the support utilities, phone, gas, power, fuel, and septic system are relatively low key on the site, they may merit some treatment to reduce their visual presence should the building be converted to educational use. The relocation of the fuel tank off-site would be necessary from an aesthetic and safety standpoint.

As the nation's principal conservation agency, the Department of the Interior has responsibility for most of our nationally owned public lands and natural resources. This includes fostering sound use of our land and water resources; protecting our fish, wildlife, and biological diversity; preserving the environmental and cultural values of our national parks and historical places; and providing for the enjoyment of life through outdoor recreation. The department assesses our energy and mineral resources and works to ensure that their development is in the best interests of all our people by encouraging stewardship and citizen participation in their care. The department also has a major responsibility for American Indian reservation communities and for people who live in island territories under U.S. administration.

NPS D-80 May 2004

Cane River Creole National Historical Park

Oakland Plantation, Gin Complex

Historic Structure Report